HELP IS JUST AROUND THE CORNER

How Love Inc. Mobilizes Care for the Needy

VIRGIL GULKER

with KEVIN PERROTTA

Creation House
Strang Communications Company
190 N. Westmonte Drive
Altamonte Springs, FL 32714
(407) 869-5005

Dedication

For my wife, Kathy, and our two precious daughters, Emily and Laura. They have shared their husband and father with so many communities. This book is for them with all my love.

Acknowledgments

BOB AINSWORTH, former World Vision vice president for field projects, once observed that Love Inc. is distinctive because it has no heroes. This ministry is composed of thousands of anonymous Christian servants who share His love with people in need. Other unheralded Christians provide quiet yet vital support for Love Inc. They are involved not for personal acclaim but to exalt the name of Jesus.

Let me tell you about just a few of the people involved in Love Inc.:

Anyone who has spent more than ten minutes with me knows the name of my wife, Kathy, and has seen pictures of our two daughters, Emily and Laura. Their willingness to make sacrifices has made this ministry possible.

Mary Tuinsma's remarkable skills as Love Inc.'s

executive secretary have been so important to the ministry and to me. I have also treasured her encouragement and her keen sensitivity to the Savior's will for Love Inc.

Kevin Perrotta has done a masterful job of clothing the Love Inc. story with the fabric of this book. It is my great pleasure to have his name on the title page.

Phil and Nancy Miller have given indispensable financial support for Love Inc. More importantly, they have provided personal support of Kathy and me. Their care and concern have carried us through some difficult situations.

The Mustard Seed Foundation gave a miracle gift. I am deeply grateful to the foundation trustees, including Bob and Carol Russell, miracle workers and friends.

Syndicated religion writer Michael J. McManus used his column to share the Love Inc. vision throughout the country. He writes with language that cares.

So many writers, including Sandra Aldrich (*Christian Herald*), Lisa Perlman (Associated Press), Dave Brannon (*World Vision* magazine), Phyllis Ten Elshof (*Christianity Today*), Steve Howell (*Worldwide Challenge*) and others have written articles that have prompted so much interest in Love Inc.

The current board of directors, chaired by Warren Waters, and the former boards have studiously maintained the spiritual and financial integrity of the organization.

The couples who comprise the founders' club have supported Love Inc. with their prayers, encouragement and major financial gifts. Many of these couples were the first to see the vision and they have embraced it with their love.

Creation House has given Love Inc. a wonderful opportunity to challenge Christians worldwide to get involved in ministry to the poor. Special thanks to my editors, Bert Ghezzi and Deborah D. Cole, for making the publication process a happy experience.

The love for the poor exhibited years ago by the Holland-Zeeland churches who participated in the first Love Inc. program has spread across the nation. Love Inc. is their gift to the churches and the poor in America.

Love Inc.'s relationship with World Vision is yet another gift from God. Special thanks to Bob Ainsworth and Craig Hammon of World Vision and Neal Berghoef of Love Inc., the architects of the plan to link the organizations.

I would also like to thank Alan Doswald and Steve Reid for their outstanding work as regional trainers for Love Inc. Special thanks also to Kathy Busse and Peter MacKinnon for their help in developing a Love Inc. training center in Chicago.

I will always praise God for the program directors, boards of directors, office volunteers, church contact people, church volunteers and all the people who participate in the Love Inc. ministry nationwide. God bless them all!

Most of all, I give praise and thanks to Jesus. He is Love.

Contents

PART 3
LOVE INC. TODAY AND TOMORROW

Foreword

THIS IS A BOOK to warm the heart, because it proves repeatedly—through the examples the author weaves throughout—the power of God's love when people of faith break out of themselves and minister personally to those in need. We have come in contact with the sacrificial life of the Savior and rediscover the essence of His statement, "It is far better to give than to receive." Perhaps there is no more important sentence in this entire book than Virgil Gulker's assertion that "if we wish to see God, we should look at the point where a caring Christian intersects with a person in need." That has been my experience over my many travels to the Third World, where I have met and been blessed by the many saints in remote corners of the world. I have met people living their faith, who have discovered that the more they

9

have given of themselves the more they have gained, not of material possessions but in the accumulation of priceless inner personal experiences and relationships. Dr. Gulker vividly demonstrates that this rich life-expanding experience doesn't have to be limited to those called to the foreign mission field; in fact, it can and should be the normative experience of every believer, each in his own community.

The author puts the primary responsibility for responding to the poor and suffering squarely on the shoulders of the church, a responsibility that has over the last forty years been reassigned to the government. The author believes that God's people want to be involved; they want to be engaged in living out the gospel in meaningful ways. He points to many examples where sincere efforts on the part of individuals and churches have taken place, some with marked success, but in many cases people in the pews simply don't know how to reach across the boundaries of poverty; they don't seem to feel they have opportunities to respond to human need within their own limitations, or they are intimidated by past failures.

This is a book that not only identifies the problem but provides a very practical solution, one that doesn't overtax pastors or depend on laying guilt trips on church members. The author suggests solutions that are manageable, even within the limited available resources of the poorest church. Yet it is a program that has a phenomenal, proven track record, with over fifty communities and over 1,500 churches currently participating enthusiastically. It is a grass-roots, Christ-centered, practical approach that involves the church in new and exciting ways to address the needs of the poor within the community with a high assurance of success. Most importantly, it opens great opportunities for evangelism with a tangible expression of the love of Christ on a one-to-one basis.

In the parable of the wise builder, Jesus challenged His followers with a very simple formula, "He who believes in Me and hears My word and then does it, is like...." If the church is to become the salt it was ordained to be, particularly in light of the limitation of governmental resources and our society's headlong rush toward materialism, Dr. Gulker's message is one that the church must not only hear, but then step out in faith to do. Here is a refreshing new approach that offers unlimited possibilities. It is an idea that I believe comes through the Holy Spirit.

Ted W. Engstrom
President Emeritus
World Vision

Introduction

*Little children, let us stop just saying
we love people; let us really love them and
show it by our actions.*

1 John 3:18, TLB

BILL KNEW I WAS TRYING to mobilize church members to help people in need. In his view, I might as well save myself the trouble. "The churches in this city are doing *nothing* to help the homeless," he declared with weary finality.

Bill was the director of a shelter for the homeless. A month earlier his comment might have expressed rage at what he saw as the church's betrayal of its calling to meet needs. But too many homeless people, too many sleepless nights and too many violent encounters with

13

frustrated clients had replaced anger with fatigue. He was facing complete burnout.

"The churches are not helping me at all," he continued bitterly. "They just don't care."

I struggled with the temptation simply to agree with this exhausted servant and go on my way. Who needs this grief? I wondered, as I glanced at the door. Why not just put my arm around Bill and have a good cry about how useless the church really is?

But I couldn't do it, because I didn't believe it.

"Listen, Bill. If I could visit every church and talk to every Christian in this city, I would ask them one question: Can you name one homeless individual or family? Precious few would be able to give me a name. They just don't know any. And they don't know, Bill, because you're not telling them."

A long, uncomfortable silence followed.

"You give them needs, Bill, but you don't give them people. You tell them how many homeless people there are, how many people and families need your shelter's services; but you don't involve them. You ask them for money, food, prayers, but you don't give them a manageable part in meeting personal needs."

More silence.

"Bill, it may well be that the church does not respond because you won't *let* it respond."

I BELIEVE THAT CHRISTIANS *do* care about the needs of people around them—elderly people who can no longer completely care for themselves, single parents who need material assistance and personal support, people who are disabled, unemployed, homeless. But I am also convinced that the structures of church ministry often frustrate individual church members' desire to show their concern. Helping agencies fail to give most Christians the opportunities, training and encouragement to care for others in the name of Christ. Church members often do not know those who are in need because church professionals, with a small cadre of volunteers, get in the way by their very efforts to serve. But with the right connection and a little help, many Christians are willing to venture forth to show the love of Christ to those in need.

This is my belief. It is also my experience. Since 1976 I have worked with an organization called Love Inc. that seeks to make the connections between church members and those in need. Over and over I have seen Christians rise to the challenge of meeting the needs of their neighbors when the needs are made specific and manageable. From Holland, Michigan, where Love Inc. began, to Bradenton, Florida; Fresno, California; Fairbanks, Alaska; and many other communities nationwide, where Love Inc. is now in operation, Christians are demonstrating their eagerness for ministry.

This book is not mainly about Love Inc. It is mainly about the tremendous potential of the body of Christ to respond to the needs of people in our society. The featured characters in the story are the individual men and women, followers of Christ, who are reaching out to show His love to their neighbors. Love Inc. exists solely to foster *their* engagement in ministry. As I will explain, Love Inc. does not help anyone. Church volunteers do all the helping.

My purpose in writing this book is twofold. First, I want to show where the roadblocks to ministry are and how they can be removed. Second, I want to tell about church members who are serving their neighbors in the name of Christ, to illustrate the tremendous range and potential effectiveness of Christian caring. My hope is that many fellow Christians will want to follow the trail they are blazing.

The structure of this book can be explained simply. The first part explores the ways that churches and agencies presently attempt to meet people's needs—and shows how 1) many needs fail to be met, 2) most church members are never involved, and 3) pastors and agency staff workers experience considerable frustration. Part 1 also tells how helping agencies and churches in Holland, Michigan, came to grips with these patterns of ministry and conceived a pilot project for an entirely different approach to involving Christians in caring for those in need.

The second part shows how person-to-person Christian caring can go beyond the help that agencies, religious or secular, can usually provide, by penetrating to the roots of people's needs for self-respect, confidence, living skills, friendship and hope. Part 3 describes the expansion and future prospects of Love Inc. and draws conclusions about how Christian ministry must be structured if large numbers of church members are to find their places in the ministry of the body of Christ to a hurting world.

At the conclusion of the book there is an appendix

which offers a checklist for examining ministry in your own church. You might want to use it as part of a group evaluation. A second appendix explains how Christians can work together to establish a Love Inc. clearinghouse in their city.

Between the chapters, you will find stories of Christian love in action. I hope these stories inspire many other Christians to hear God's call to put their time and talents together with His power and reach out to those around them who are in need.

The stories are true but the names and some minor details have been changed in order not to reveal the identity of persons involved.

THE POSSIBILITY THAT the body of Christ can actually minister to the many people in our society who are in need is an exciting one. Charles Colson has written eloquently about the multiplication of efforts by ordinary Christians to care for those who are hurting. "God's platoons" he has called the bands of Christians which have appeared in recent years to minister to prisoners, to women with crisis pregnancies, to the homeless. The demands of church members *insisting* on being given a place in the ministry of the church may be one of the most formative trends in the churches in the coming decade. The challenge today is not to create such a movement—the Holy Spirit is creating it—but to remove the obstacles and build the linkages between ordinary church members and needy neighbors.

One man who has glimpsed this vision is Bill, the former shelter director. Beneath his cynicism about the churches, he had a desperate need to find out that what he was saying about the churches' irrelevance to needs was not true. When he saw evidence that church members *can* be involved in caring for the needy, he reversed his approach. As program director of Love Inc. in his city, Bill now devotes himself to throwing open the doors for church members to enter into ministry and giving them the support they need to walk confidently through them. I hope that this book will help many other Christians glimpse that vision and discover the opportunities for ministry in their own churches and communities.

PART 1

Removing the
Obstacles to Ministry

Hot Tub Christianity in the Far North

NEIGHBORS ON A STREET in Fairbanks, Alaska, may be wondering why the same woman visits Martha Howard's house early each weekday morning. The visits seldom last more than fifteen minutes, but they occur as regularly as clockwork. Martha's visitor is Sandra Olthuis, a volunteer from a nearby church. Each morning she helps Martha, whose joints stiffen up overnight because of arthritis, to get out of bed and into a hot bath. Once Martha is in the tub, her joints begin to loosen up, and Sandra says good-bye. Martha is able to dress herself and go off to work.

ONE

Christians:
Keeping Their Distance

PICTURE THE HOUSE three doors to the right of your own. Or the apartment three doors down the hall from yours. Do you know who lives there? What are their children's names? (Do they *have* children?) What's on their minds this week? What difficulties are they facing? What needs do they have? Simple questions—but questions many of us cannot answer.

There are various reasons for our ignorance. Neighbors come and go before we have a chance to get to know them very well. Life is busy. People often keep their weaknesses and problems to themselves. And so we often do not make contact with the people around us who might need our help. The folks in one home stagger under a burden too heavy to bear, while others of us nearby go about our lives unconcerned—because we are unaware.

For some people, this is fine. "I live my life; you live yours" is just the way they like it. But if Christ lives in us by faith, our failure to make contact with those who are in need can be a source of deep frustration. God has poured His love into our hearts by His Holy Spirit. We want to serve. It saddens and angers us— and makes us feel guilty—to think that people around us are suffering in ways that we might alleviate, only we do not know who they are or what we might do.

I once received a letter from a woman who wrote: "At Christmas I saw hundreds of poor, starving people on television. But I realized that I didn't know a single truly poor person and I had no means of getting in touch with one. If God was giving me a heart for the poor, He would need to show me how I could do something for them." Like this woman, many Christians have a "heart for the poor." They want to show Christ's love to people in need. But their good intentions remain dammed up behind a barrier of not knowing—not knowing who and not knowing how.

What would happen if it were possible to break through that barrier and release the waters behind it?

I must admit, this is not the way I always looked at the absence of most church members from Christian ministry. Some years ago I worked for a church-supported helping agency in Holland, Michigan, called the Good Samaritan Center. We were constantly seeking volunteers to run the programs we set up for children with reading disabilities, elderly people, those with sight and hearing impairments, and others. Volunteers were not easy to come by. Far from seeming like a vast reservoir of care-givers, the churches seemed like a desert. Finding helpers for our programs involved laboriously sinking wells and hoping to strike water. My question was, Why don't Christians care?

But a conversation with a local pastor got me thinking about the matter differently. Late one afternoon I was tidying up papers on my desk when the pastor of a church that contributed money to our center walked in. I asked him to sit down, and he inquired about how things were going. After a few minutes he leaned back and said, "You people are doing a great job responding to needs for us. I'm sure our church would be willing to enlarge our financial support to cover some of your other programs. You know, it's so difficult to get people in our church mobilized to do anything. Maybe you should take over our evangelism program too."

I protested that evangelism was an essential part of church life—how could any church turn it over to an organization to do for them? But the pastor was unconvinced. "I'm sure you would do a better job than we do ourselves."

Praise can sometimes be more uncomfortable than criticism. After the pastor left, I turned his suggestion over in my mind. On the one hand it seemed ridiculous. If a church got us to evangelize for them, what would they ask us to do for them next? Pray and do their Bible reading for them?

Still, his proposal made an odd kind of sense. If church members could rely on our center to act on their behalf in the service of needy people, why *shouldn't* they also hire us to evangelize on their behalf? Is helping needy people less central to the mission of the church than preaching the gospel? Don't the two go hand in hand?

And, then, if there is something faulty in a church turning over evangelism to an outside agency, isn't there something less than ideal in turning over the care of needy people? If our agency shouldn't do church members' evangelizing, should we be reaching out on their behalf to people around them with various physical and emotional needs?

The pastor saw us as successful. We were caring for people in need. But it dawned on me that what he admired in us was a questionable kind of success. He saw the Good Samaritan Center doing what his church members seemed unwilling or unable to do. But our success in helping needy people meant accepting the failure of the great mass of church members to reach out in service to the many people with all kinds of needs who lived nearby.

An agency like ours was a middleman. On one side were people with all kinds of needs—needs for housing or food, for help getting through some crisis in their lives, for someone who would take a personal concern for them. On the other side were church members— uninvolved, apparently uncaring, but with some money to offer. Our center was in between. We took money from the church people and provided services to the needy. We were in between on the churches' behalf. But now it struck me that we were also in between as a barrier. We were separating church members from those in need. Our organization shut off the church members from contact with the people in need, even from the very people their money was serving. And the better we did our job, the more effective a barrier we became. Our success made it less and less necessary for church members ever to have anything to do with needy people in person.

I realized that, while we were helping a lot of needy people, we were not helping the church. Indeed, we might be one reason the church's caring potential seemed so small. We were used to thinking that most church members did not care. But how could we tell how much they cared if we constantly put ourselves in between them and suffering people? Agencies like ours had become a kind of McDonald's of charity for church members: "We do it all for you." Perhaps, hidden behind the barrier we had erected, there really was an untapped reservoir of Christ's people ready to help those in need.

THIS LINE OF THINKING spurred me to look around and try to understand how churches relate to people in need. As I travelled and talked to pastors and church members, I discovered several models that churches use for showing mercy to the people around them. These are the main approaches that I found:

1. **Support helping agencies.** Through their financial contributions, church members support the Good Samaritan Center and countless other religious and secular agencies. The approach is not all bad. Money is inevitably needed to some degree. So is the professional expertise that agencies offer. But the model

provides little opportunity for love to grow between the church member who is giving and whoever it is that is in need. Consequently, church members lack the interest and motivation that come from knowing *particular* persons who need help. Instead of visiting and serving elderly Ruth McKinley in her home once a week, or regularly driving disabled George Serotnik to his physical therapy sessions, church members knew only of "old people in need," "the hungry" or "the homeless."

In addition, parachurch agencies are magnets. They draw some of the most dedicated church members out of involvement in their local churches. The churches become a farm league training their best volunteers for recruitment by the major league helping agencies. But when the prime volunteers serve outside the church, the local church is left with tired, inactive leadership for its own ministries.

When churches let agencies minister for them, they end by losing any sense of their own call to minister. The director of social services in one Michigan county was disturbed by the complaint of two pastors who called on him at his office.

"Your department is not doing its job," they accused him.

The director was taken aback, since his office had an exemplary record. "Why do you say that?" he asked.

"We know," the pastors said, "because people are still coming to the churches for help!"

2. **Let the pastor do it.** He's paid to do it, many church members reason. But while the pastor may make a sincere attempt to help a needy person who shows up

at the church door, he rarely has much to show for it. He is too occupied with other responsibilities to be able to find out what kind of help the person really needs. Too often he ends up simply reaching for an envelope in his desk drawer marked "discretionary," handing the person a few dollars and sending him on his way. More often, he leaves things to the church secretary. She then has to decide whom to give a few dollars to and whom to turn away empty-handed. Either way, most church members are uninvolved.

3. **Assign a committee to help.** This is motivated by compassion, but committees are policy-making bodies, not action groups. To refer a hungry person to a committee is an act of unintentional cruelty. It could be weeks before the committee meets, considers the proposal and makes a decision.

4. **Appoint a contact person.** In most churches there are a handful of women who love Jesus a great deal and are congenitally unable to say no. If anyone asks them to help, they will, no matter how far it takes them beyond the limits of their time and resources. Some churches select one such person and refer any needy people who show up to her. She does the works of mercy for an entire church—in some cases even for a church that numbers in the thousands.

5. **Hire an outreach worker.** Invariably the job description of a professional outreach worker employed by a church says that this person "will facilitate the involvement of the body of Christ at such-and-such a church in ministry to the needy." Everyone assumes that simply publishing such a statement and hiring

someone to fill the position automatically involves church members in ministry. Not true. The outcome is usually the same as with a volunteer contact person: one person struggles to serve, while many do not serve at all.

6. **Set up a food bank.** This has become quite popular. Many churches that used to help supply secular agencies' food banks have set up their own. But few churches carry out research to ascertain the need for a food bank prior to developing one. And without such investigation and coordination with local agencies, a food bank can actually do more harm than good. By channeling resources away from agencies that are most accessible to needy people, the new food bank can create a food *shortage*.

Church food banks often operate without attention to nutritional needs. They simply offer what church members decide to donate. If it were not for food drives at church, some of us would never get rid of our cans of kidney beans or okra. Many church food banks are run at the convenience of the church rather than the convenience of the hungry: hours are by chance or appointment—like an antique shop. I have even known pastors who have refused to divulge the location of their church's food bank because it is a "discretionary" enterprise. (I am not sure I even care to know what that means.)

Another problem is that setting up a food bank can give a church a false sense of confidence that it is doing its share to help needy people, while, in fact, serious needs may be going unmet and only a few church members and church resources may be engaged in helping the needy. I know of one 2,000-member church, with an $11-million endowment, located in a high-need, downtown area, whose only community outreach is its food pantry, staffed by a mere handful of volunteers. Yet ask anyone in that church what the church is doing for the needy, and they will tell you about the food pantry.

A more subtle but equally damaging problem is that a church that focuses its ministry to needy people on a food bank can be seen as an adjunct of the secular welfare agencies. The church focuses on needs rather than on persons and loses distinctive person-to-person ministry in the name of Christ.

Churches' efforts to set up clothing and furniture distribution services often suffer from similar problems, especially a disregard of people's actual needs. Church members give items that they want to get rid of rather than those that are most needed. In defense against such careless care, one such service emblazoned over its door this motto: "If you would give it to Jesus, we'll take it."

7. **Holiday food baskets.** This is the extreme form of help that serves the giver rather than the receiver. Food baskets have very little to do with compassion. Compassion involves understanding and meeting people's needs, while food baskets have mainly to do with assuaging feelings of guilt. Church members spend eleven months storing up guilt, then discharge it at the holidays by giving food baskets.

I have known pastors to call an agency at Christmas for names of needy people and afterward complain because church members saw food in the cupboards of people to whom they brought baskets. Did they expect to find folks who ate only once a year and sat patiently the rest of the time, waiting for church members to bring holiday food baskets? Obviously the church members were motivated more by a desire to feel good than a desire to help. The more destitute the recipients, the more satisfaction the givers felt.

One pastor stopped by my office at 4:00 p.m. on Christmas Eve with his wife and children, bringing a turkey. He had planned to make a family ritual of giving a meal to a poor family. Instead of making arrangements ahead of time, he assumed there would always be a needy family available for whom he could care at his own convenience.

8. **Training.** Various organizations offer seminars and workshops training church members to minister to the people around them. Some programs offer real wisdom. The problem is that they offer theory divorced from practice.

They are like my first instruction in swimming. When I was a boy, a friend of mine who was an excellent swimmer got me interested in learning to swim. "That's great," I said to him. "Next summer I'll sign up for the beginners' course."

"That's not necessary," he said.

"Why not?" I asked.

"I'll teach you," he said.

"Where?"

So he taught me how to swim—on the garage floor. Under his direction I learned all the motions. But the next summer when I dived into a real pool, I almost drowned!

Many training programs are like that. They say the right things, but they do not put church members in contact with flesh-and-blood needy persons. Learning to minister becomes a substitute for ministering. People learn a helping skill, such as how to offer budget planning, but have no way to be in touch with people who need what they have to offer.

ALL THE APPROACHES I found in churches had common problems. The paramount shortcoming is the failure to involve many church members in meeting the needs of fellow human beings. Institutions, staffed by a few individuals, do almost all the work. The arrangement stifles the maturing of church members' love. The church should not only be *teaching* members that faith should lead on to love (James 2:14-26), but should also be *creating the opportunities* for them to put faith into action. The church should articulate the teaching and then facilitate Christians' carrying it out. But the usual arrangements for helping the needy remove opportunities from church members, reserving those opportunities for a corps of professionals and a small number of others. Church members are deprived of their privilege, their birthright, to minister ''to the least of these.''

As a result, needy people remain distant, unknown. Suffering people remain nameless and faceless, a mass ''out there'' who do not activate our sense of personal responsibility. When the waters of caring are dammed up indefinitely, they become brackish. When we lack direct contact with people's pain, their needs become merely one item on our agenda—and not necessarily an important item. Other considerations crowd out the priority of helping those in need.

Once in a discussion with a group of pastors about how to bridge the gap between church members and folks in need, a pastor told me, "That's fine, just so long as my people won't have to interact with immoral people." Another pastor protested, "We do evangelism only," implying that Christians can share Jesus Christ without "mixing it up" with people who are in pain. Responses like these come more easily the more distant we are from the people in need.

When the needy person is only an idea or a cause, his or her pain is easily dismissed. One church was asked to decide whether they would sponsor a Vietnamese refugee family. They formed a committee and debated the issue at great length. Finally they reported back the recommendation that the church not sponsor this family, and that the refusal to sponsor should be interpreted by the Vietnamese government as a protest against their invasion of Cambodia. The committee was totally detached from that refugee family. No real people figured in their debate, only concepts. Thus ministry shaped by distance between church members and the needy is fatal to those in need.

When needy people are distant, the precise nature of their suffering has little impact on the church. The church goes its accustomed way, offering the services it finds easiest and most congenial, rather than those that are most urgently needed. Or it gets caught up in the excitement of someone's wonderful idea, without taking the time to determine whether there is a need for what is proposed. Without conducting any research, one church thought it would be a good idea to set up a home for girls caught in the court system. But they received no referrals and had to sell the house. Another church recruited foster parents for abused children. But no foster children were referred to them and the network disintegrated. Meanwhile real needs in the community went unmet.

The church often reminds me of a college professor I asked to help prisoners at a jail in Miami. The prisoners were poor Latin American women who had been offered $100 or so by agents of drug rings to take flights into Miami carrying little packages. The women were not told that the packages contained drugs. Customs officials discovered many of them and marched them off to jail—many of them mothers of children and not able to speak a word of English. I was involved in educational work at the jail, and I approached the professor to see if he would teach survival English to these women. They needed a simple vocabulary—words like aspirin, babies, phone call. After a couple of weeks I got a complaint from the staff. The man was taking the women through a college course in English, beginning with grammar. He did not see the women's desperate state and could not adapt his help to their needs. The church is often like this—doing what it is used to doing, whether or not that happens to help people where they are hurting. (Simple language instruction took a step forward at the jail when the administration arranged for the matrons, who were also not appreciating the women's problems, to reverse positions with them for a few hours. The prisoners, who spoke only Spanish, stood out in the corridors, while the matrons sat in the cells and tried frantically to communicate. The exercise did wonders to raise the matrons' consciousness about the prisoners' situation as their need for a toilet increased and they desperately mouthed, "Bathroom, bathroom, bathroom!")

Ministry models that maintain distance can lead to unconscionable neglect. Consider these cases:

• One December when I worked at the Good Samaritan Center an extremely successful businessman called and said, "I know a young woman who needs your help. She has no place to live, she has no funds, and she has no family or friends. Will you help her?"

"Mr. Boyle," I said, "before I address this young woman's situation, I would like to tell you how impressed I am that in the midst of all your responsibilities you are calling around to see if you can get help for her."

"Thank you," he said.

"One other question," I said. "May I ask your relationship to this young woman?"

"Certainly," he said. "I evicted her last night."

He had no awareness that he had any responsibility for her. Accustomed to current models of church ministry, he simply assumed that someone else would take care of her. Since he contributed fifty dollars per year to the Good Samaritan Center, he believed that the woman's need was my job.

• A mother with a baby and other young children was living one winter in a decrepit house. The landlord refused to make repairs because he wanted to demolish the building. Some of the windows were out, and the house was drafty and cold. I made an urgent appeal to a nearby church for clothing. The people at the church said they would look into it. Several days later when I called back, the person I spoke to asked, "Couldn't you find another church to help?"

• A young woman attempted to commit suicide. After she received emergency counseling, I telephoned a pastor. "This woman is home now," I explained, "and she has asked to see a pastor. Could you visit her within the next few hours?"

"Absolutely," he replied.

But he got so caught up in committee meetings that he forgot. That night she tried to commit suicide again.

• Another young woman, this one a single parent with several little children, asked a pastor one Sunday, "Is there anyone in your church who could help me be a better parent?" The pastor's response: "We don't do that sort of thing here."

• In my six years of working in prisons more than a decade ago, I came across fewer than five Christian volunteers. Some church members once explained to me that it was perfectly reasonable for Christians to ignore most of those who are in prison. When Jesus spoke about visiting prisoners (Matt. 25:36, 43), they claimed, He meant only visiting people who are in prison by reason of their profession of Christ.

The thread that runs through all these stories is that

people have been conditioned to ignore each other. Ministry arrangements constantly shield church members from real people whose lives are in crisis.

Our common ways of ministering follow the tendency in our society to institutionalize people with needs. Needy people make us uncomfortable. So we put them in institutions. What distinguishes the contemporary church from the Jews who neglected the injured man in the story of the Samaritan is that we have set up institutions to attend to the dead and dying for us and have learned to avoid certain streets, neighborhoods and kinds of people. And even when they are not institutionalized, we expect some program to meet their needs. This way we do not have to acknowledge their personal existence.

The attitude is epitomized in the response I have gotten more than once when I have asked a fellow Christian to help someone in need: "Doesn't the welfare department do that?" We end by making ourselves so emotionally distant from people in pain that we can look on them without seeing them. I vividly remember a street scene in Chicago: an ageless, white-haired, disheveled woman wandering along a crowded street carrying a baby blanket and sucking her thumb. Many people jostled her as they hurried past, but no one paid any attention to her. Their indifference rendered her as invisible as if she had been miles away behind a mental institution's blank walls.

MY INVESTIGATION INTO how churches meet the needs of people around them was sobering. Most church members had only a vicarious experience of Christian ministry. It was not that there was no love in the church, but people had no means to express it. Ministry models based on distance between church members and those in need were a formula for hopelessness for hurting people: there was never enough help.

I joked to a friend that we could express the churches' lack of person-to-person service by designing a vending machine that could be installed in the rear of any church. Needy people would get whatever help they needed by pushing a button. One button would dispense help; another button would dispense help with a tract. No church member need ever be involved. Don't use the joke, my friend cautioned me. Word of such a machine will get around, and you're sure to hear from some church wanting to know where they can buy one!

Surely, I thought, there must be a better way.

The Biker and His Baby

ACE'S WILD LIFE in a motorcycle gang screeched to a halt when his girlfriend abandoned him, leaving him with their six-month-old baby. To his surprise, fatherhood took hold of him. A sense of responsibility slammed the brakes on his wandering ways.

Ace arrived in Denver homeless and jobless. Through people he met at a shelter he heard about Love Inc. and called. A church volunteer listened carefully to his story. The volunteer asked Ace what he would choose to do if he could have any job he wanted. Because he couldn't read well, Ace eliminated a lot of possibilities. Finally he replied, "I'm a good handyman. I'd like to be an apartment manager. If I could do that, I would have a home for my baby and be able to work close by."

The Love Inc. volunteer mentioned Ace to his wife. She, in turn, told her women's Bible study of his situation. One of the women responded that her husband owned an apartment complex and was looking for a manager. It did not take long to put the two men into contact with each other.

Today, several months later, Ace is working as an apartment manager. He has a home and child care for his baby. Through the concern of a network of Christians, God has given him the chance to make a new start.

TWO

Agencies:
Treating Symptoms

F ROM MY FRUSTRATION a plan emerged. If the
basic problem was that church members were cut
off from the needy people around them, the solution
would involve bringing them together. If most church
agencies unintentionally kept church members apart
from needy people, perhaps a different kind of organization could put them in touch with one another. I
wondered what such an organization would look like.
How would it identify people with all their different
kinds of needs? How would it link them with the particular Christians who would be able to help them?

The churches themselves, I decided, were not the best
place to find the answers. They were not on the front
lines. In most cases they did not know what the needs
were. While they sometimes developed enthusiasm for
serving, their enthusiasm would wane, and they would

disappear. As an agency director I would receive occasional visits from church groups that had gotten charged up by a sermon or discussion about "needs" or by an annual message about "discovering your spiritual gifts." The visitors would want information about senior citizens or some other group to help. We would provide the information. A response was seldom forthcoming. Enthusiasm alone is not enough to generate involvement.

In order to build a model that would fit the requirements, the people to consult were the folks at the helping agencies in town—the welfare department, the community mental health center, the migrant workers organization, and the rest. They were in the trenches. The churches talk a good game, but the agencies play it. So I made the rounds of the agencies.

To my surprise I found that the agencies were not in good communication with each other. The most glaring instance of this turned up in my own office. When I mentioned to the staff at the Good Samaritan Center that I was planning to contact the city mission—an independent downtown ministry—they told me, "We don't work with the city mission."

"Why not?" I asked.

"I don't know," one staffer replied. "We had a disagreement with them. But I can't remember what it was." Nor could anyone else.

The city mission's director, like me, was new in the job. Since neither of us had any reason to avoid cooperating, we decided to meet and got along fine.

After a few weeks of one-on-one meetings with other

agency heads to get acquainted and build relationships, I called a meeting of representatives of all the helping agencies in town. Staff members from twelve agencies came, including the welfare department, the hospital, the police department, the community mental health center and the crisis intervention phone line. There were also two church agencies, which provided some excellent services but did not seem to have gotten beyond the problem of isolating most church members from most of the people in need.

It was the first time that many of these people had met. As we sat around two long tables in the basement of the city mission discussing needs and resources in Holland, Michigan, we assembled the pieces of the big picture of who the needy people in town were and what kinds of help we were giving them. The overall picture showed that our failure to coordinate our services was hurting the people we were in business to serve. The key problems that we uncovered were:

Mistaken referrals. Although an organization in our community had published a sophisticated resource inventory, it was out of date, and no one had the time and money to keep it accurate. As a result, there were gross inconsistencies between what each of us thought other agencies did and what they actually did. In our ignorance we had been making referrals for services that had not been offered for weeks, months or even years.

For example, we would refer people needing relief for utility bills to a certain organization, not knowing that the organization's funds for this purpose were generally depleted in the first two weeks of the month.

We would send people needing rides outside Holland—say, to medical appointments—to another agency, not knowing that they provided only local transportation. We would send people needing groceries to a third organization, without taking into account that agency's inability to consider clients' special dietary needs.

I offered the story of a man who walked into my office with his hand held out, saying to me, "I'm here for the $100." He had been sent by an organization which told him that I would give him $100. Hand still out, he repeated his statement.

"But I don't know who you are," I said, "or what your need is." My refusal simply to give him money upset him. This was understandable. The other agency had led him to believe that I would automatically alleviate his need in this way.

Abandoning people in bureaucratic mazes. Sometimes, we found, we referred people to the right agencies but failed to give them the help they needed to navigate the complex process of applying for assistance.

For instance there was the case of a woman with degenerative bone disease. She came to see me only when the advance of her disease forced her to cut back to part-time employment. Her job was some miles away, and her car, like her body, was wearing out. She would not be able to work much longer. What would she do then? She was getting desperate.

I referred her to the Social Security department to ask about eligibility and find out the amount of help she might get. The next day she returned to my office, stooped over and grim-faced. She sat down without saying anything and handed me a note—a suicide note. I knew something must have gone wrong at the interview. I asked her if she would go back with me to the agency. After five minutes with the man she had spoken with the day before, *I* was ready to commit violence— on the man who was interviewing her. He was so protective of federal funds that he projected a total lack of concern about her plight. It took an intervention on my part over the following days to get the information she needed and steer her through the application process. She couldn't make her way successfully through the system by herself. She needed an advocate.

The problem is not unusual. Getting help can be difficult, even when a person has a legitimate need and has made contact with an agency that is designed to meet that kind of need. An acquaintance of mine with twenty-two years' experience working for the welfare department decided to go through the application process for assistance to see what it was like. He gave up without reaching the end. He found that the forms were too complicated for him to complete!

Unfortunately, none of our agencies provided advocacy to get through each other's application processes. Our mistaken referrals and daunting procedures meant that vulnerable people were sent to places where they did not end up receiving help. Discouraged, many of them eventually stopped asking. Thus in some cases we were consigning people to perpetual need.

Failure to get at the real needs. The help a client needs is often deeper—and different from—the help he or she requests. For example, clients often ask for

47

financial assistance, even when they have needs that money won't meet. The focus of agencies on giving money contributes to this problem. People tailor their requests to fit what they think agencies want to give them, just as job applicants tend to color their job history to accord with what prospective employers are looking for. It might be that what people really needed was job training, literacy skills, psychological counseling, help to secure child support payments or instruction in how to set up a budget.

We agency people acknowledged that service providers deserve to be called professionals only when they demonstrate the ability to sift the requests of clients and penetrate to the root causes of their problems. But we also acknowledged that we were so overloaded that we often lacked the time to make a determination of actual need. We were responding to the most urgent, superficial needs, not to the whole persons who came with those needs. We were treating symptoms.

Supporting chronic dependence. I detailed for the other agency people what I perceived as my successes, describing my dealings with a dozen individuals and families. Then I asked the other agency staff people to tell about some of their successes. We were astonished to find that we had many of the *same* success stories. Unwittingly we had been helping the same dozen people to perpetuate a life-style of dependence.

There was Don, for example. He presented himself as an ex-convict, and he was. But from that point he left facts behind and roamed in the realm of fiction. His standard story was that because of his criminal record no one would hire him. He claimed also to have a physical ailment, which varied between a stomach disorder or a foot problem, depending on the situation. He would go to pastors, claiming to be in town for the first time. However, he refused to stay in a mission shelter and insisted on being put up at a particular motel. I have since discovered a fair amount about Don. I can go into any community in my home area of Michigan and describe Don's *modus operandi* without mentioning his name, and both agency folks and pastors will immediately say, "You mean Don!" He ranges throughout Michigan asking for financial help. The prison he says he was incarcerated in varies, from Jackson prison, when he is seeking charity in southern Michigan, to Marquette prison, when he is looking for handouts in the North. He always carries sufficient cash to prevent being arrested for vagrancy, and he maintains a post office box in one Michigan town where he receives disability checks from Social Security.

There was Mary Jo, from Hammond, Indiana. She would make a very emotional appeal concerning the death of her mother, which created various needs, including money to go to the funeral. I have since learned that Mary Jo concentrates on smaller, more remote communities in Michigan. I have documented the "death" of her mother on at least three occasions.

And there was Debbie, who made a convincing appeal for help for her two children. She always insisted on regarding the money given her as a "loan." She could even persuade people who had been informed of her ploy. A pastor who had been warned about her once called me from his study and said he had Debbie and her children there and he was about to give her some money. He told me how miserable the children looked. I told him to examine the dirt on the children's faces, and he would see that it had been applied in a definite pattern.

These people had settled into a lasting, irresponsible dependence on other people. Some of them had learned to manipulate the system very deliberately. But we could not say that these people were simply lazy or dishonest. We agency people had to recognize our share of responsibility for the life-style we had constructed for them by our own policies. We were at least partly to blame because we reinforced their chronic dependency.

For example, our sharing at the meeting revealed that several agencies gave away clothing. The duplication was actually convenient for the agencies. In Holland there was no shortage of donated clothing, and so there was no reason to ration its distribution. Imposing more accountability on the distribution of clothing would reduce distribution and thereby produce a stockpile of clothing. This would require renting a warehouse. In addition, controlling distribution at each agency and coordinating distribution among the agencies would take a lot of time. The agencies saved money and time by simply giving away clothing to anyone who asked. But, one agency representative pointed out, it was apparent that some people were showing up at one agency after another asking for clothes. It turned out that some of these people simply never did laundry. When clothes got dirty, they threw them away and went back for more.

After all, if you don't have your own washing machine, why go through the bother of going to a laundromat, as long as clean clothes are always available?

Who was responsible for this behavior? Surely the agencies contributed to it by their own irresponsible style of compassion.

The same was true of financial aid. Whenever assistance is readily available, people will take advantage of it and may not even think they are acting irresponsibly. Why should a person feel guilty about accepting something that an agency or church readily provides? (An especially memorable instance of financial irresponsibility was a client's request that a church donate money to pay his fine for welfare fraud!)

It was incredibly frustrating to realize that our way of doing things unintentionally kept people focused exclusively on their physical needs. We made it virtually impossible for them to achieve any level of self-esteem, because the helping experience was not designed to give them the help they really needed to become self-sufficient; it was geared to meeting their needs for clothing, money or whatever, in the manner that was simplest for us. Much of the blame for chronic dependence lay with the service providers, who lacked the resources and relationships with other providers to intervene more deeply in their lives. The system was betraying people.

THE AGENCY REPRESENTATIVES reached the decision to work together more closely. In a series of meetings in the fall of 1976 we systematically gathered information about needs and resources in the Holland area. We conceived of a clearinghouse that would interview people to determine their needs and would refer them to the appropriate agencies for help. We developed a policy statement for the clearinghouse and even came up with a name—Love Inc.

We agreed that the clearinghouse:

• should not promote any further duplication of efforts in town;

• should conduct a need analysis of each client to determine the nature, extent and legitimacy of his or her needs;

• should identify people who were chronically dependent, not with the intention of dismissing their needs but in order to understand their whole need and to involve them in the process of overcoming their irresponsible behavior;

• should confirm the availability of help at an agency before referring someone to it.

Helping agencies would work cooperatively in analyzing people's expressed needs. The clearinghouse would become a city-wide data bank on people having a wide variety of needs.

The next question was how to use the clearinghouse to bring these needy people into direct contact with church members. I suggested to the agency people that the clearinghouse could be used to connect needy people not only with appropriate agencies but also with church members who could help them. Doing this, I argued, would be a way of enlisting more people, more resources, in helping needy people in the community.

The agency staff members were not optimistic about this proposal. Their general view was that the churches were irrelevant to meeting needs. Staff members cited instances in which churches had unnecessarily duplicated services or had started out to provide help but then lost interest. Agencies expressed their sense of responsibility to protect their clients from church members' passing enthusiasms. They were interested in asking churches for food, clothing and money, and even for volunteers for programs. They did not, however, envision making the churches partners with them in helping the needy members of the community.

One reason agencies did not perceive a need for church members was that the war on poverty had produced a multitude of organizations and funding streams. Agencies had appeared to meet every need. The proliferation of well-funded agencies for a while masked the fact that agency efforts unfortunately often did not alleviate the needs or eliminate poverty. The spending cuts of the 1980s would force agencies to cast about for new resources. The possibility that church members might be enlisted became more attractive as it became clear that they represented not a reshuffling of existing resources but an infusion of new ones.

In any case, in 1976, despite reservations, the agency workers admitted that a cooperative program with church members would be great if it worked.

The next step, then, was for me to go to the churches.

A Long Day,
An Astonishing Year

I KNEW IT WOULD BE a long, difficult day when Jim stormed uninvited into my office. He looked as worn, tired and angry as he had the last time he stormed uninvited into my office.

"You've got to help me," he demanded. Before I could ask why he needed help, he blurted out the same kind of sad story I had heard from him so many times before. He had lost his job. He and his family would be evicted in two days if they didn't pay their rent. His wife was ill, and he could not afford medication for her. In addition, the department of child protective services had threatened to remove their two children from the home because of parental neglect.

"You've got to help me," he repeated, a quaver in his voice betraying fear and confusion beneath his anger.

"It's no good, Jim," I responded. "You've come to

the well too many times.''

He tried to interrupt, but I talked through his inter-ruptions. ''Listen to me, Jim. You've hit nearly every agency in town over and over again. You've lost at least six jobs and four apartments in two years. Protective services wants to take your children again because you're not providing food for them. If you don't pay your rent, you may not even be able to provide hous-ing for them. You can't expect to get any more hand-outs from agencies in Holland, Michigan, until you assume some responsibility for your own needs.''

Jim was furious now. His demands for food and money were punctuated by the profanity of a man who sees no escape from imminent disaster.

When I was finally able to calm him down, I told Jim that I wanted to help him help himself. ''I will recruit a volunteer family from a church to act as a support system for your family. The volunteer family will share budget planning, tutoring, menu planning, house clean-ing, child care and any other skills you and your wife need in order to make it. But I will set up a family sup-port system for you on one condition: you have to find a job.''

''That won't help,'' Jim screamed as he shot up from his seat and stormed out of the office. ''I'll kill my kids before I let anyone take them!'' he yelled over his shoulder as he slammed the door behind him.

Throughout the day as various agencies connected with the Love Inc. network were contacted by Jim, they routinely checked with me as part of an interagency need-analysis procedure. In each case I told the agencies what I had told Jim: I would involve his family in a support system if he would locate a job. Each agency told him he should come back to talk with me.

Late in the day Jim returned to my office. "What did you mean by that support system idea?" he asked. Having spent his anger, he was coming face to face with the realization that he would have to participate in the solution to his problem. I repeated what I had told him earlier.

Within forty-eight hours Jim had found a job. I then called a contact person in a church near his home to arrange for a volunteer family to work with Jim's family.

A year later, after many hours of effort by the volunteer family and by Jim and his wife, the results were astonishing. At that time I made the following observations:

★ Jim was still employed. This was the longest he had ever worked at any job.

★ The children were happy, healthy and receiving adequate care.

★ Jim's family had become independent of agency support.

Significantly, the volunteer family had spent only fifteen dollars in the course of the year-long family support experience.

THREE

Pastors:
Needing a Plan

FALL 1976 WAS MY SEASON for meeting pastors. In Holland, Michigan, where churches outnumber taverns, there is one pastor for every 500 people. But, as in other cities across the country, not all of them get along with each other. I would have liked to invite all the pastors in town to an evening's discussion about the needs of our neighbors and how we could help. But I reluctantly conceded at the outset that some pastors would not be enthusiastic about meeting with those of other denominations. I would best involve them in the vision for city-wide cooperation in caring for the needy by meeting with them in small groups, and even one-on-one. In any case, my focus was not on breaking down denominational barriers or developing ecumenical ministry, but on opening the way for church members to serve in the name of Christ. Large group meetings could wait until later. And so, day after day for several months, I made my way from parsonage to rectory until I had talked directly to seventy-eight clergymen in the Holland area.

With one pastor after another I shared the proposal that had evolved from the meetings with agency representatives. I wanted to help each church conduct an inventory of its human helping resources, I explained. If the churches identified members willing to provide various services, the clearinghouse would connect them with clients who needed their particular services. All the pastors listened with interest.

With many of them, the point at which I captured their imagination was when I spoke about churches reaching out to the people in their neighborhoods. I had marked the location of every church in Holland on a map, with a zone around each one (see page 61). "Look," I said. "Every church is in a neighborhood. I suggest that your church assume responsibility for the needs that arise in your church's neighborhood. I am not going to ask you to respond to needs in another country or another state, or even across town. I am talking about sending your way people who are hurting right in the shadow of your steeple."

Many organizations, I pointed out, seek to enlist the support of Christians for ministry to needy people in faraway places. Helping organizations such as World Vision and the Catholic Bishops' Relief Fund use the picture and story of a hungry child "out there" to elicit our support. They bring that distant person right into our living room in order to make a financial appeal.

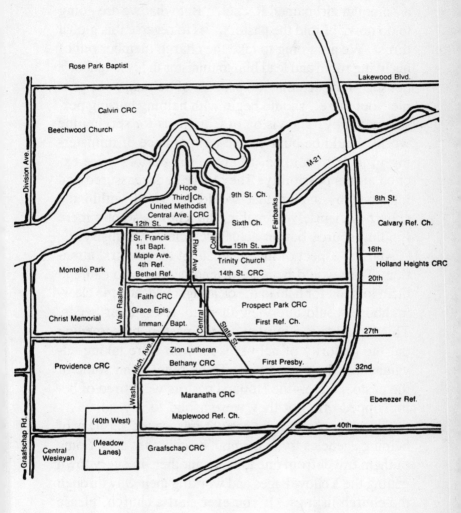

Church Zoning Map
Holland, Michigan
February 1980

Rose Park Baptist

Lakewood Blvd.

Calvin CRC

Beechwood Church

Division Ave.

M-21

Hope
Third Ch.
United Methodist
Central Ave. CRC
12th St.

9th St. Ch.

8th St.

Fairbanks

Sixth Ch.

Calvary Ref. Ch.

St. Francis
1st Bapt.
Maple Ave.
4th Ref.
Bethel Ref.

River Ave.

Coll

15th St.

16th

Montello Park

Trinity Church
14th St. CRC

Holland Heights CRC

20th

Van Raalte

Faith CRC

Grace Epis.

Imman. Bapt.

Central

Prospect Park CRC

First Ref. Ch.

Christ Memorial

State St.

27th

Providence CRC

Mich. Ave.

Zion Lutheran

Bethany CRC

First Presby.

32nd

Wash.

Maranatha CRC

Maplewood Ref. Ch.

Ebenezer Ref.

Graafschap Rd.

(40th West)

(Meadow
Lanes)

Graafschap CRC

40th

Central
Wesleyan

61

Through just such a program my own family supports a Zambian girl named Rachel. "But what we are going to do now," I told the pastors, "is to reverse this global thrust. We are going to take the church member *out* of his living room and lead him to minister in his neighbor's house." I argued that the process of helping poor people "out there" should begin with helping hurting persons close by. The vision of Christians for serving the world should be built on their experience of ministering in their own town. Many of the pastors were excited at this possibility. They were both reassured and intrigued by a plan that would be based within the churches themselves, making the churches not a mere funding source but an actual vehicle for ministry.

Another aspect of the plan caught the pastors' attention. They would be able to send people who came to them looking for help to the clearinghouse, and the clearinghouse would interview them to assess their needs. This would take a burden off the pastors by screening out the minority of help-seekers who were taking advantage of their good will. To be blunt—and some of the pastors were—the Holland pastors were tired of being ripped-off. But they were afraid to say no.

The same people who seek to misuse the services of helping agencies try to manipulate churches also. Some of them travel from one town to another, in every town getting the Yellow Pages and working their way through the church listings. (If you ever start a church, please don't choose a name that begins with A. If you call yourself the Apostolic Assembly of Anytown you are right at the top of the panhandlers' list!) In a city I visited recently, I was interested to notice that the church section of the Yellow Pages had been torn out of the phone book. Other abusers of the system will choose a denomination and stick to it throughout a trip. At one period a person may be a staunch Lutheran, stopping in at all the Lutheran churches; next year he may be Christian Reformed. The theological versatility of some people is unbelievable. In one West Coast city, police recently broke up a ring that bilked thirty churches of thousands of dollars with appeals for rent money. The proceeds supported the group in an unsavory life-style that involved illicit sex and drugs.

Without screening, the pastors had no way of knowing whether the person asking for help was also getting help elsewhere—or whether he or she needed help at all. Most pastors did not have the training to evaluate the genuineness of the stories of those requesting help. And even if they did, what pastor could take the time to do it? With sermons to prepare and meetings to attend, with sick members to visit and weddings and funerals to perform, pastors did not have the time to sort out what was going on with all the people who came to them.

Not surprisingly, I discovered that pastors had been helping the same dozen chronic abusers of the system that the agencies had been supporting. Some pastors, if they suspected double-dealing, would give only a little money. Other pastors had progressively narrowed down the range of people they would help. At first they had given financial help to anyone who asked. Then, having been burned, they restricted their largesse to those who attended the church. When this did not eliminate irresponsible requests, they further limited their giving to members and then to those who tithed. Lacking a system, they had progressively redefined their commitment to care. The clearinghouse's assessment of clients' needs would protect pastors from the problem of unscreened, questionable requests for help.

Finally, like the agencies, the pastors suffered an underlying anxiety that stemmed from knowing that they were rarely able to deal effectively with the real needs that people brought to them. They patched a lot of wounds but helped few people regain their health. Helping just one person might take several days' effort. Lacking the time, the pastors dispensed small amounts of money. But they knew that often the clients' basic needs could not be solved by money alone. The pastors were invariably dissatisfied with dispensing quick fixes of this sort. One pastor told me with frustration that his church had been giving money to certain families for years without seeing a fundamental improvement in their situation. The plan for coordinating church and agency efforts and for involving church members with a range of skills offered the prospect that needy people would get more than band-aids.

From my many conversations with the pastors I strongly sensed that they wanted a system that would accurately analyze people's needs and would involve their church members in meeting needs safely and responsibly. The pastors saw the necessity of having a structure to accomplish this, and they were willing to be persuaded that the evolving plan I presented might do the job. All those I spoke with decided to join the plan.

We agreed that the clearinghouse would assess the needs of individuals seeking help and would refer them to the churches, and the churches would try to find church members to help. Each church would provide one or two contact persons, whom we would train to identify church members that would help. The clearinghouse would guarantee that when we called a church the people we referred would be members of that church or residents in its zone. We would also assure the church that the clients had an authentic, specific, manageable need.

While the pastors were all willing to try the plan, they had two reservations. First, some were doubtful that church members would help. And second, they were doubtful that the agencies in town would cooperate.

"Funny," I told them, "that's exactly what the agencies said about you."

Finding New Friends Along the Freeway

THE RED OIL LIGHT on the dashboard of Roger's aging station wagon blinked on. Almost immediately a grinding noise shook the car. The engine stopped, cutting off the power steering, and Roger wrenched the disabled vehicle to the side of the freeway. The car rolled to a halt. Roger turned to his wife and said, "I'll take a look." Getting out, he raised the hood and examined the engine. He stood back and looked at the marooned station wagon sitting at the side of the freeway. It pretty well summed up where his life was going: nowhere.

Roger and Joanne had come from homes torn apart by family conflict. When they married in their teens, they did not seem marked for success. Their situation became especially precarious when Roger lost his job about the time their baby was born. After searching for employment in their area of Southern California, he

67

decided he should explore elsewhere. They were driving north to no certain destination when the car quit.

After trudging silently down the freeway to the outskirts of the nearest town, they came to a motel, and Roger took a room. The manager of the motel took note of this young couple with a baby. Roger made unintelligible responses to her questions, but Joanne offered a little information.

The manager knew about the local Love Inc. office. She called the local program director and told her about the young family. "They need food, and milk for the baby," she said. "But they need more than that. They need someone to help them figure out what to do."

The Love Inc. director located Janet, a church member, who drove over to the motel to meet Roger and Joanne. Roger was polite but, again, not talkative. Joanne was happy to have someone to share their situation with. Janet took an immediate interest in the baby, and the two women were soon deep in a long discussion of babies, food, public assistance and jobs.

This was the beginning of a friendship between the two women. The next day, at her own expense, Janet took Joanne grocery shopping. Over the next week or two she helped Roger make contact with county social services. After some time, he was able to get some financial help. He eventually went through some testing and qualified for job training as a truck driver. In the months that followed, Janet and other volunteers helped get Roger and Joanne moved into an inn where they could stay more cheaply.

Janet's friendship made a big difference for Joanne,

as she and Roger faced successive difficulties. Joanne became pregnant, but the baby was born prematurely and required extra care. Roger completed truck driver school, but couldn't find work as a driver. Janet was a calm, confident presence in Joanne's life.

Recently a small apartment became available at a cost that Roger and Joanne could afford. "I'm scared," Joanne told Janet. "What if we can't make it financially? What about furniture? We don't have anything. It would be so nice to be settled in an apartment, but I just don't know if we can do it." Janet assured her that the Lord would help and sent out a request through the Love Inc. network. Church members provided a refrigerator, a love seat, beds and other basic items the family needed.

After a couple of years, Roger is beginning to relax his reserve and distrust. He never let anyone but himself and Joanne care for the children, even for an hour. But Joanne has just had her third child, and the day after the delivery Janet came to the apartment and handed Roger her car keys. "You go see Joanne at the hospital," she said, "and I'll watch the kids for a couple of hours." Roger took her up on it.

Not everything for Roger and Joanne is straightened out. They have arguments. Joanne, who is only twenty years old, gets overstressed caring for their three small children. After a second round of vocational testing, Roger qualified for financial assistance to enable him to receive training to become a nurse, but it will be some time before he finishes nursing school.

Janet and the other church volunteers who have aided them through Love Inc. have not revolutionized Roger's and Joanne's lives. But they have helped change the demise of the couple's station wagon from a dead end into an opportunity to get them moving in the right direction. The volunteers have had some occasions to say something to the couple about Jesus Christ. And Janet was especially touched last week when Joanne told her that she wanted to begin giving baby formula and paper diapers that she didn't need to some other family that could use them.

FOUR

The Clearinghouse Approach: Testing a Solution

ONCE WE HAD THE IDEA for the clearinghouse, the reality took shape almost overnight. It was like staring at a mass of jigsaw puzzle pieces for a long time, and then suddenly seeing how they fit. Once you see where the pieces match up, it doesn't take long to put them together. The meetings with the agency representatives began in September 1976. In October, even before those meetings ended, I began visiting the pastors. By the end of October we were training the first contact people assigned by churches. In November the contact people were conducting surveys in their churches to discover available talents. The clearinghouse opened its doors and was making referrals by the end of the year. Thus by the beginning of 1977 the basic model for what has since become Love Inc. was in operation.

Here, in brief, is how the system works, whether in

Holland, Michigan, or in any of the more than fifty other communities where chartered affiliates of Love Inc. now function.

Preparations in the churches. Each local church that joins the program selects one or two members as contact persons. Love Inc. trains them and provides them with survey forms listing common needs of people in the area, developed in conjunction with local helping agencies (see page 73). The surveys are need-oriented rather than interest-oriented. The purpose is to discover who in the church can provide services that are actually needed, rather than to find out merely what church members might like to do. Most churches allow the contact persons some time during worship on a Sunday morning to explain the program to the members of the church and distribute the survey forms. Having the contact persons conduct the survey on Sunday morning helps to identify them in the minds of the church members with the Love Inc. program. Members fill out the surveys, indicating what they are willing and able to do, and the surveys are collected at that time. (Some contact people joke that they've locked the doors and windows until all the surveys are handed in!)

The survey results are organized into a talent inventory in the church. A summary of the results is sent to the local Love Inc. office, where it becomes part of the clearinghouse's city-wide inventory. The Love Inc. office does not get the specific names of church members, because then churches might be tempted to eliminate the contact persons and let Love Inc. do all the work. That would negate the purpose of spurring churches to

TALENT TITHE INVENTORY

LOVE INC. has asked that members of local churches become involved in responding to individual and family needs which arise, or currently exist, in the area surrounding their churches. Our church has agreed to participate in this program because we believe it will give each church member a precious opportunity to put his/her Christian faith and love to work in the service of those in need.

LOVE INC. will refer neighbors with legitimate and manageable needs to the trained contact person from our church. This contact person will give you the opportunity to provide the service you indicate on this inventory.

Name _____

Address _____

Phone _____ Age _____

NOTE: If you are unable to help when called upon, you may simply decline that request.

Available Hours: (please check)

	Morning	Afternoon	Evening		Morning	Afternoon	Evening
Mon.	_____	_____	_____	Fri.	_____	_____	_____
Tues.	_____	_____	_____	Sat.	_____	_____	_____
Wed.	_____	_____	_____	Sun.	_____	_____	_____
Thurs.	_____	_____	_____				

I AM WILLING TO VOLUNTEER IN THE FOLLOWING AREAS:
(Please Check)

____ Assist with shopping one or two times a month

____ Assist people in filling out various forms

____ Transporting people to medical appointments one or two times a month

____ Deliver food occasionally with adequate notice

____ Visit shut-ins, elderly, disabled or handicapped __ once __ more often

____ Visit and encourage people who have no family/friends to help them

____ Respite care for single parents or those living with handicapped persons

____ Companionship for elderly

____ Transport furniture in your truck

____ Do yard work for disabled and elderly

____ Share skills: __ auto __ appliance

____ Translation help Language _____

____ Counselor

____ Medical asst. ____ Legal asst.

____ Dental assistant

____ Money management counseling (we will train you)

____ Plumbing ____ Carpentry

____ Painting

____ Provide short-term emer. housing

____ Provide housing for unwed mothers

____ Meal planning

____ Tutor adults (we will train you)

____ Tutor children (we will train you)

____ Donate baby supplies or furniture

____ Temporary baby-sitting or child care

____ Financial aid (for rent, utility bills, medicine)

____ Be a caring friend for someone who is alone

____ Other talents, skills, interests and helps you want to contribute: _____

_____

P.S. I may be willing to serve one or more shifts as a phone volunteer in the LOVE INC. Clearinghouse. (Shifts are 9 a.m.-noon or 1 p.m.-4 p.m., Mon.-Fri. Training provided.) Please contact me with details.

PLEASE RETURN TO OUR LOVE INC. CHURCH CONTACT PEOPLE

_____   _____

discover and mobilize their own resources for ministry.

Operations at the clearinghouse. To illustrate the process, let's follow the stories of some fictional but typical clients:

• Roger Binkowski, a retired machinist, is seventy-three years old and has diabetes. Five years ago the advance of Roger's disease necessitated the amputation of both his feet. Now his doctor has told him that he needs dialysis twice a week. This will mean two round trips in a special vehicle that can accommodate his wheelchair, at a cost of $100 per week—far beyond his financial ability.

A neighbor of Roger's asks his own pastor if the church can help. The pastor calls Love Inc.

Phone calls by Love Inc. staff to Roger and the hospital validate the need. He *does* need the treatment and does *not* have any way to manage the transportation.

The next step: find an agency that can provide the service or locate the resources within the churches. In Roger's case, no agency is able to help. So Love Inc. draws on its bank of information about churches with members who are willing to drive patients to and from medical appointments. A few phone calls to church contact persons locate several church members who are willing to drive. The big challenge is to find a church that has a van with a wheelchair lift. After some inquiries a church is discovered that has the right type of vehicle, which it uses to take nursing home residents for recreational rides. With some schedule juggling, the church is able to make the van available at the times when Roger needs to get to and from the hospital.

Love Inc. puts Roger, the volunteers and the church with the van in touch with one another and coordinates a schedule. The following week, Roger begins dialysis. Week by week, Love Inc. checks with the church contact persons involved to find out if the schedule of rides is being maintained and to see whether the volunteers are running into any problems.

• Richard and Marilyn Naylor knew they had a financial problem. The electric company sent them a notice that it was about to shut off their power because their payments were so long overdue. The Naylors heard about a state agency that might provide assistance and went to get help. The agency was able to draw on a fund to make a one-time utility bill payment, and this averted the immediate problem. But the agency representative could see that without additional help the Naylors would soon be in the same predicament again. And so he advised them to call Love Inc.

The Love Inc. program director asked what kind of help they needed. The problem, as the Naylors saw it, was that they simply did not have enough money to meet their expenses and Richard could not find a better-paying job than his present one. When the program director asked for details, Marilyn brought out a grocery bag stuffed with bills and collection notices. She could not say how much they owed. The couple simply let creditors take payment directly from Richard's paycheck and lived on what was left over. Some weeks that was very little.

The Love Inc. director went away doubtful that the Naylors needed more money but certain that they needed help managing their money. Through the communications network with local churches she found Don and Carol McGill, an older couple who were willing to help the Naylors sort out their financial situation and learn how to establish and stick to a budget.

Through follow-up calls over the next few weeks, the program director learned that the McGills had discovered a further unsuspected problem: the Naylors were virtually illiterate. Consequently they were unable to read the bills and other letters they received from businesses they owed money to. Richard and Marilyn were surprised when the McGills pointed out that this was surely a key factor in their inability to control their finances. With the McGills's encouragement, they enrolled in adult basic education classes. After a few months, with the McGills's continuing advice, Richard and Marilyn felt that they were getting control of their money for the first time in their married lives. The McGills reported that they experienced the prayer support of a prayer group they belonged to as crucial for their efforts to minister to the Naylors.

• Harry Kessler was a familiar visitor at most of the church offices in town. For years he had managed a precarious, alcoholic existence on the basis of handouts and odd jobs. At the time that a Love Inc. clearinghouse was set up in his town, Harry was following the local shelter program night by night as it rotated from one church to another.

However, the shelter program was closing down for the summer, and Harry began making the rounds of pastors asking for money. They referred him to

Love Inc. On the basis of an interview and the information supplied by the churches, the program director had what diplomats call a "frank and honest exchange of views" with Harry.

"Harry, the kind of help you're looking for is not the kind of help you really need," she told him. "What you need to do is begin to take responsibility for your life. I can help you do that. I can find you a job and a place to live. But if you're not willing to take a steady job, none of the churches working with Love Inc. will give you any more money. So what are you going to do?"

"I don't want your help finding a job," Harry snarled.

Harry went away in a huff, and the program director did not hear from him again. But a few weeks later a pastor called and asked if Love Inc. could find some furniture for Harry. It seems that Harry had continued visiting churches without success, and after a while of sleeping outside and scrounging for food, he met a pastor who made him the same kind of offer that the Love Inc. program director had made. This time he was ready to accept it. The pastor found him a regular job, and Harry was letting the pastor handle his finances for him. The pastor also found Harry an apartment, and now hoped that some furniture could be found.

Phone calls to churches and agencies in town brought offers of all the basic items that Harry needed. Volunteers from the St. Vincent de Paul Society picked them up and delivered them to Harry's new home.

EACH CLIENT IS UNIQUE. Each person's needs are different. But in every case the Love Inc. clearinghouse follows a four-step process (see page 79).

The first step is **receiving information about a need**. A call might come from a pastor or church contact person, or from a staff worker at an agency. Or the needy individual might call or come in person to the Love Inc. office.

The second step is **making an assessment of the person's needs**. Sometimes, as in the case of Roger Binkowski, this is a fairly simple matter of verifying that the person does in fact need what he or she says. At other times the original description of the need turns out to be mistaken. An agency asked Love Inc. to arrange help for an elderly woman who was living alone and was not eating well. The report was that she needed help learning how to cook. On investigation, however, it turned out that she had raised several children and knew perfectly well how to cook. Her problem was that she was so lonely she did not want to eat.

The needs assessment is important because people in crisis are often poor judges of their own needs. Perhaps they are developmentally disabled or are bewildered by a traumatic event such as abuse or desertion, or lack living skills, such as money management. Like the Naylors, a client may be acutely aware of a particular need, but there may be something more that he does not see. As a result he asks for the wrong kind of aid or does not ask for what he needs most.

The helping person's job, then, is not just to supply the need that impinges on the client most directly, but to walk the client through the analysis process so that the client himself can see his situation clearly. The

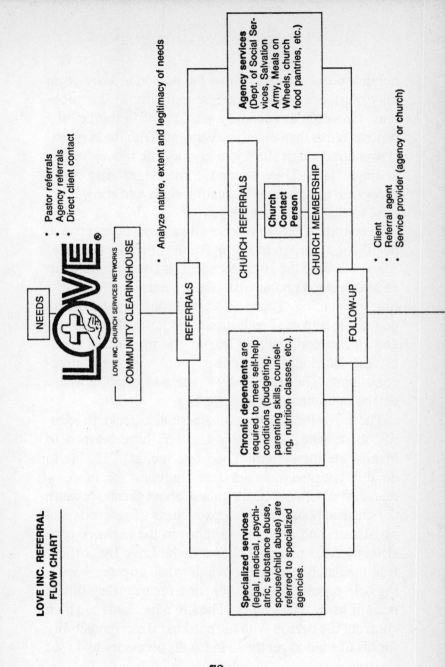

LOVE INC. REFERRAL
FLOW CHART

NEEDS
- Pastor referrals
- Agency referrals
- Direct client contact

LOVE INC. CHURCH SERVICES NETWORKS
COMMUNITY CLEARINGHOUSE

- Analyze nature, extent and legitimacy of needs

REFERRALS

CHURCH REFERRALS

Church Contact Person

CHURCH MEMBERSHIP

Agency services (Dept. of Social Services, Salvation Army, Meals on Wheels, church food pantries, etc.)

Chronic dependents are required to meet self-help conditions (budgeting, parenting skills, counseling, nutrition classes, etc.).

Specialized services (legal, medical, psychiatric, substance abuse, spouse/child abuse) are referred to specialized agencies.

FOLLOW-UP
- Client
- Referral agent
- Service provider (agency or church)

79

helping process should allow the person to learn from his experience and assume responsibility for his problem. He needs to become a participant in the helping process rather than merely a recipient. With the Naylors, it was not enough simply to give a little money to pay a single bill. They needed someone to help them recognize their lack of budgeting skills and show them how to handle their money.

Every client falls somewhere on a continuum between healthy interdependence and unhealthy dependence. Those closer to the interdependent end of the continuum need direct aid and advice. Their needs tend to be less time-consuming. Those who are chronically dependent on outside help need education to understand their needs and an apprenticeship in learning to meet them themselves. Working with these people is more time-consuming. The needs analysis seeks to pinpoint where on the continuum each client lies.

The Love Inc. needs assessment also seeks to identify those who, like Harry Kessler, have learned to manipulate the system. The Love Inc. staff is able to do this because agencies and churches are in communication with the clearinghouse about clients, because the clearinghouse itself keeps records of referrals and assistance, and because churches in the network consistently refer potential clients to the Love Inc. office. It immediately becomes obvious when anyone is seeking help repeatedly, whether for a recurrent legitimate need or using a fake story. The Love Inc. staff can then confront the person with his need to take responsibility for his life and to get the living skills necessary to do so.

On the basis of the needs analysis, the Love Inc. staff moves on to step three, **referring the person for help or securing help from church members**:

• If the person has a specialized need, Love Inc. makes the referral to a specialized organization. It might be a need for dealing with spouse abuse, a legal need, a medical or psychiatric need. If the person requires an existing good or service provided by an agency like the Salvation Army or a food bank or clothing closet, it makes the referral to that organization. We pledge to helping agencies that we will not knowingly ask a church to duplicate an existing service.

• If the person needs some kind of help not provided by an agency, Love Inc. turns to the church. If the client is a church member, we go first to the person's own church. But more than eighty percent of all our clients have no church affiliation. These we refer to one of the churches in the zone where they live.

Because of the analysis process, the Love Inc. staff can guarantee the legitimacy of the need. We can also be specific. We do not tell the church contact person there is a need for people to help an elderly man who is sick; we tell the contact person that Roger Binkowski, who lives a half mile from your church, needs someone on Monday and Thursday mornings from 9:30 to 10:30 to drive him to and from Mount Carmel Hospital, and the job requires some lifting.

The Love Inc. staff workers are able to put what they know of the need together with what the resource inventories tell them about church volunteers in churches in the area. So when they refer a need, they have good reason to be confident that the church can meet it.

If the client's situation is complicated, the Love Inc. staff breaks it down into its parts. Rather than asking a church if "someone could help elderly Mrs. Wellington," the staff explains that Mrs. Wellington (1) needs to be driven to the grocery store, (2) needs someone to help her go through the process of applying for public assistance, and (3) needs living room and bedroom furniture. Different volunteers could take on different tasks. Each volunteer can succeed at his or her task. No one need be overwhelmed. Love Inc. is trying to create a secure context for ministry, within which success is virtually guaranteed, rather than throwing church members into situations which are further opportunities for failure.

It does sometimes happen that a need comes our way which we do not think church volunteers can handle. In that case, we do not refer it. I was once asked whether we could find a volunteer to drive a client from a state mental hospital to an appointment with a physician. "Is there a possibility of risk to my volunteer?" I asked.

"I am not at liberty to divulge that information," the agency representative replied.

"Well, would it be wise for two people to perform this service together?" I asked.

Again the representative responded, "I am not at liberty to divulge that information."

"I'm sorry, then," I told her, "but I can't help you." The agency representative was furious. But we are very conscious of the fact that church volunteers are not social workers and that we cannot treat them as though they were.

• We tell chronic dependents that they must meet self-help conditions appropriate to their needs. Generally, Love Inc. will ask churches to help a client financially only once without setting the condition that the person accept budget counseling or even, in some cases, third-party handling of their money. The person is told that if they opt not to accept that condition and participate in meeting it, then Love Inc. will no longer ask the churches to help. Love Inc. does not say to a client, "No, we won't help you"; we say, "Yes, we will help you, but there is a condition you must meet." (Chickie Hansen, program director in Buchanan, Michigan, quipped, "Love means never having to say, 'I'm sorry. I can't help you.' ")

Individuals have not always been delighted with the self-help conditions that we have imposed on them. One father told me he would not accept a job because he would not deprive his family of his presence. Clients have advised me to do some rather peculiar things with my conditions. But conditions do work. They do help people learn to help themselves. Clients who initially refuse conditions often return later when they are serious about coming to grips with their personal and social needs. In Fairbanks, Alaska, Love Inc. declined to give an alcoholic man further assistance. Six weeks later he returned and reported that he had gotten sober. He thanked the staff for refusing to respond to his request. Their refusal, he said, helped him face up to the reality of his situation.

Sometimes people will say, "You're a Christian. It's

your *responsibility* to love me.'' At that point we have to say how we define love. To care as a Christian does not mean simply dumping money. It means making an investment in a person's life. It may mean helping a person find a job, teaching him to handle money, showing him how to be a good parent. We explain to the client that our attempt to impose self-help conditions on him, to teach him to help himself, expresses the love that we feel. If we felt no love for him, we would simply give him the assistance he requests, without getting involved in his life.

If the individual refuses to fulfill the self-help conditions, we do not arrange further assistance. No individual can be forced to help himself, no matter how desirable or necessary that goal may be from our perspective.

All clients are referred outward. Everyone who comes to Love Inc. with a real need and a willingness to cooperate with whatever self-help conditions may be imposed is sent to an agency of some kind or is connected with church volunteers. The Love Inc. staff does not help anyone.

This is not because we don't want to. Sometimes we are very tempted simply to help the person ourselves. But if we did that, we either would be duplicating what an existing agency is already established to do, or would be getting in the way of church members' ministering to needy people. The moment we helped someone, we would become one more organization blocking the body of Christ from ministry to human needs. And so, in keeping with our agreement with agencies and churches, Love Inc. has adopted the novel slogan, ''We will not knowingly help anyone!'' Our role is to perform need analysis, make referrals, conduct follow-up and generate new church resources for meeting needs.

I am fond of the exclamation of a woman who once called Love Inc. in Muskegon, Michigan. The staff worker asked the routine question, "Has Love Inc. helped you before?''

"No,'' the woman said.

But after a quick check of the card file, the staff worker came back to the phone and said, "Our records indicate that we have helped you four times.''

"The people at the Presbyterian Church have helped me four times,'' the woman admitted. "But you people at Love Inc. will never do anything for me,'' she added in an accusatory tone.

No, indeed. The minute we start helping anyone, we have lost sight of our goal and have become part of the very problem we have set out to solve.

The final step in the process is **follow-up**. After a service has been provided, the Love Inc. staff calls the church contact person to see how things worked out. Was it a constructive and helpful experience? Sometimes when we believed we understood the need, we really didn't. Elderly Mr. Randolph not only needed someone to do his grocery shopping, he was in danger of losing his house and needed someone to help him work through his situation. Things may have gone badly. Once we found out that a volunteer was rather discouraged after responding to our request for help. She transported a client to a clinic and later discovered that the client had lice. The volunteer had to get her car deloused. It was not a problem that we could have foreseen. But once we knew it, we took a different approach to arranging help for that client.

Follow-up may be the end of a short-term service arrangement. But it may also be the beginning of longer-term Christian ministry. A follow-up call to a client offers the opportunity to create a relationship, to share about Jesus Christ, to ask if the client would welcome a visit from a church member. Often the client responds affirmatively.

It is interesting to note that the follow-up step was originally introduced into the clearinghouse format partly to answer the concern of some agency representatives that church people might be pushy about their faith and evangelize clients recklessly. The agency people wanted to make sure that neither clients nor volunteers went away from the helping experience feeling abused. Very rarely do clients report that they did not appreciate a volunteer sharing their Christian faith, and often clients express an interest in further contact with someone from a church.

WHEN LOVE INC. BEGAN operations in Holland in December 1976, there were some who told me, "Nothing this simple will ever work." But it did. The agencies liked it because they received people whose needs had been analyzed and because they benefitted from the availability of greater church resources. The churches liked it because they were treated as responsible partners in ministry. Church members liked it because they were finally able to minister.

The clearinghouse not only worked for simple needs—rides to medical appointments, someone to read to a blind man, furniture for a single mother. Christians in Holland rose to meet some remarkable challenges. One day a woman at the welfare department called. "I have a young mother of three children in my office," she said. "The youngest child, a seven-month-old, has multiple birth defects and cries ninety-five percent of the time. She has required cardiopulmonary resuscitation three times since she was born. The mother is utterly exhausted. She needs respite care, or she is going to have a nervous breakdown. Can you find any church volunteer to help?"

You can't be serious, I thought. How can I possibly go to a church with this kind of need? I did call a church contact person, though, and she was confident she could find someone to help. Soon she had a registered nurse who was willing to care for the little one. Not only that, but the church embraced the family with friendship and undertook to pay the child's medical bills.

The clearinghouse approach had tapped into unsuspected reserves of Christian caring.

The Woman Who Was Left All Alone

ONE MORNING MIKE HIGGINS stuck his wallet in his back pocket, walked out to his pickup truck and drove away. Nothing unusual about that. His wife, Dorothy, hardly noticed. What was unusual was that he never came back.

No good-bye. Not even an angry word. Just a door closing, the sound of a truck pulling out into the street, and twenty-three years of an increasingly troubled marriage trailed off into lasting silence.

Dorothy telephoned the police. There was a visit by a policewoman. A routine search. Then, for weeks, nothing. Having gestured his contempt by leaving without a word, Mike had disappeared. Finally, a few weeks later, there came a report that he was living with another woman in a trailer park in another state.

Dorothy replayed the departure scene often in her

mind as she sat hour by hour, with the television flickering in front of her. Earlier scenes—a few bright, many bitter—also returned. As day followed day and Dorothy sank into a paralysis of anger and guilt, a possible outcome presented itself to her: "Maybe I'll kill myself."

What roused her was not any call from a friend or relative (there was none around) but a letter from the landlord. Having exhausted every grace period for payment of rent, the notice informed her, she now had seventy-two hours to quit the apartment.

This jolted Dorothy into action.

She called her sister-in-law who lived across the state, and her sister-in-law gave her the name of a pastor in town. A call to the pastor yielded the phone number of Love Inc. After some hesitation, Dorothy dialed the number.

Julia, the program director, explained that a single person in Dorothy's situation could get $260 a month in welfare—but not immediately. Without any remaining funds, Dorothy would have to move. Julia would orchestrate the help she needed.

The next day a bunch of active, concerned church volunteers burst into Dorothy's life. They moved her furnishings into storage. Dorothy's silent, anguished world was whirled away, and she was driven to a motel for a couple of weeks.

Dorothy hadn't worked outside the home for years. A volunteer suggested she might be able to take a job as a caretaker for a disabled person in the person's own home. It was a new idea for Dorothy, but she was willing to give it a try. Within a week she had her first job, caring for a man with Lou Gehrig's disease. Being a mere five feet and ninety pounds, moving the man around looked like quite a challenge. But the first afternoon Dorothy had to give him an enema, and after that accomplishment, she felt she could handle anything.

Her pay was not great, and without savings she did not see how she could afford the move-in expenses of a new apartment. But a church volunteer who owned a set of apartments let her move in and pay the damage deposit over time, and another volunteer paid her first month's rent.

Then, in an auto accident, Dorothy shattered her ankle. She would be in a cast, unable to work, for five months. It was hard to pick up the phone and call Love Inc. again, but there did not seem to be any alternative.

Julia gladly arranged another round of help. Without workmen's compensation, Dorothy had no income. Volunteers provided rent, utilities and groceries until she could get on general assistance. Two men came once a week to carry her and her wheelchair down two flights of stairs and take her to her doctor's appointment.

Now, months later, Dorothy has started back to work part time. She is getting established in a new life.

Church volunteers have witnessed to her, prayed for her and waited. It just so happens that the family she is presently working for has a Bible study in their home once a week, and Dorothy has started dropping in. They have also invited her to go to the Baptist church with them, and she has gone with them the last two weeks.

Just the other day Dorothy told one of her new friends, "I know it's the Lord that has brought me through the last year."

FIVE

Christians:
Willing to Minister

A S SOON AS THE LOVE INC. clearinghouse
started up in Holland, Michigan, it began to
answer the crucial question regarding the cause of the
widespread failure of Christians to minister to people
in need. Why do so many Christians fail to help the
needy people around them: because they do not care?
or because they have not been mobilized effectively?
Do the church and civil agencies merely fill the gaps
left by church members' lack of concern? Or are church
members distant from needy neighbors because the
structures of church and agencies block them from personal contact? If a way was found to overcome the
separation between church members and people in need,
would they respond in the name of Christ?

In Holland we soon had the participation of seventy-
four churches, representing thirteen denominations and

including four nondenominational churches. Christians were getting involved in ministry and they had never had any idea that they could. In one church, seventy-five percent of the members volunteered.

As Love Inc. clearinghouses have been set up in other places, the pattern has been repeated. In Fresno, California, 1,800 Christians have volunteered to serve. In the Kenai Peninsula of Alaska, 1,300 people from twelve churches are working to meet needs. And the Christians who are volunteering come from all kinds of backgrounds—young and old; those who are well-off and those who might generally be considered candidates to receive ministry; poorly educated people who have never been asked to minister before and highly educated professional people, such as doctors and lawyers, who have previously lacked a responsible way of making their services available. We quickly demonstrated that Christ's people *do* in fact want to care.

This is not what most people, including pastors, expected. They looked at the existing evidence—only a small percentage of Christians actively engaged in ministry—and they concluded that the desire just wasn't there. In view of the evidence, their conclusion was plausible. Why, then, were they mistaken?

From the experience of Love Inc. we can now identify at least seven factors that contribute to the failure of Christians to reach out to people in need:

1. **We do not entrust people with important ministry.** A pastor once said to me, "It doesn't make sense for me to try to find volunteers in my church for meeting needs outside the church. I can't find enough

people to keep the church machinery turning. If I can't get anyone to cut the church lawn, what makes you think I could get someone to cut some old person's lawn?'' The pastor overlooked the fact that cutting the church lawn is not a high ministry calling that attracts people. His difficulty getting members to care for the church's property was not a good guide to the response he might have gotten if he invited them to minister to people in need.

2. **We don't involve church members in giving service in the wide variety of ways that might interest them, fit their schedules and use talents they are confident of.** Some pastors feel protective about the busy core of lay people who do most of the jobs in their churches. The pastors are reluctant to ask them to take on yet more services to needy people outside the church. They do not want to put additional pressures on them. What the pastors fail to consider is that the invitation to care for neighbors' needs may be just the ticket to activate many of the church members who are not doing much right now.

Charlotte Reeves, the program director of Love Inc. in Bakersfield, California, once pointed to a church in her town with more than 1,000 members and recalled that the pastor held back from joining the Love Inc. network because he didn't want to overburden the 150 or so members who are involved in ministering in the church. ''The other 850 people,'' Charlotte observed, ''might very well be willing to do something on Tuesday morning or Saturday afternoon, outside the regular church programs. We want to reach the people in the church who are not doing anything, who don't feel qualified to carry out existing ministries.''

3. We don't inform church members sufficiently about needs. Ask the members of almost any church to identify the three primary needs in the neighborhood of their church, or even in their town, and you will rarely receive a well-informed answer. Most church members will tell you what they read in the newspaper or saw on television, but that is often national or global. They do not have a focused awareness of the needs of the people who live close by. The reason is that those of us in charge of church helping programs have not made it our goal to inform them. Consequently, church members lack the motivation that would come from having a clear idea of what needs to be done.

4. We don't present needs in personal terms. Pastors too often burden their congregations with recitations of vast needs: thousands of homeless over here, millions starving over there. They offer vague exhortations to feed the hungry, support the aged, and so on. No one can respond to such general exhortations. We have to translate mass needs into individual terms. We have to personalize it. Jesus did not send His disciples to heal 18,000 paralytics and 20,000 blind people; He gave them the example of caring for people one by one.

What Christians need is invitations to help particular persons with particular needs. When I was with the Good Samaritan Center, I learned that it did little good to ask churches if they could ''supply tutors for learning-disabled children.'' The request was too broad. Once, however, we asked if there was anyone who could help a little boy named Johnnie. We told church members that he was a fourth grader who was unable to read and, because he could not read, the other children made fun of him and would not play with him. I was amazed at the response. It seemed as though everyone wanted to tutor Johnnie. We had to tell volunteers that we were sorry, but Johnnie was already being helped. Perhaps they would like to help Becky or Kimberly learn to read? (They did.)

If I come to a church and say that there are many people in nursing homes who have no family, no friends, no one to visit them, it is extremely unlikely that the next day anyone will go to a nursing home and say, "I want to see someone who doesn't get visitors. Send me to their room and I will spend some time with them." Most of us are too insecure to step out like that, even though we might want to. But if I were to go into a church and say, "Mildred Simpson is an elderly blind woman living at White Oaks Home down the road. Her whole family lives out of state, and she hasn't had a visitor in a year. Would anyone care to drop in on her on Tuesday or Friday afternoons to read to her?"— why, I would have to beat the volunteers off with a stick.

5. **We don't facilitate person-to-person contact.** Without personal contact, it is hard to sustain the motivation to help. Giving money, collecting food and clothing—people's enthusiasm for such things flags if they rarely see the needs of the person who is being helped and what difference the help makes. Most churches suffer a pattern of no personal contact, leading to no enthusiasm, leading to no available resources.

Putting church members into direct contact with needy people begins to reverse the pattern. The commitment to care grows enormously when, instead of an abstract need, the church member is helping a person with a name and a face.

6. **We don't break needs down into manageable parts.** As I visit different churches, I repeatedly hear the request, "Make it something we can handle. Give us manageable needs, and we will respond." The idea of helping Mr. Kendricks, the alcoholic retiree in the apartment house next door, get his life together is overwhelming. The request to drive him to a doctor's appointment is manageable.

7. **We don't build people's confidence.** Christians want to serve, but often lack the confidence to step out and do it. They need a structure that makes it look manageable, ensures them success at the start and encourages them to believe they can do it. Isn't that what Christian leaders should be doing?

One of the most powerful experiences I have had of the impact that confidence can make took place some years ago in a Florida college where I was asked to work with three young men who were taking remedial courses. I was informed that they were virtually illiterate. But I suspected that their reading skills were higher than the college authorities thought and that the conviction of the authorities that the men couldn't read was part of their problem.

At our first meeting I said, "I want you men to help me pick out the books for the reading class I'm going to be teaching. I want each of you to read ten books this semester and give me a report on whether any of them would be suitable for the class.'' All they had been given to read in college was diagnostic stuff—very gray and boring. I took them to a paperback distributing company. They were amazed at the colors and variety. They picked out ten books apiece. The next day when I arrived to work with them, the three men were already sitting reading. ''Mind if we just read for a while?'' one of them asked. Over the next few weeks every one of them read ten books and gave me a report on each one. More importantly, they asked to assist me in setting up a paperback library in a local jail.

The parallel with the church seems clear. We need to treat members with confidence that they do have gifts for serving, rather than communicating the view that only a few, highly trained people are qualified.

This will require a revolution in how some pastors think about their members and about ministry to people in need. I often think of a woman from my church many years ago who went around asking whether there was anyone she might help. She was referred from the leader of one committee to another, and no one thought she had anything to offer. Finally she said to me, ''I have been to all these groups. I wanted to help someone, but I guess what I'm being told is that with only seven years of school, I am not qualified to help.'' This woman had raised nine children, one of whom had Down's syndrome. She had a marvelous store of basic living skills. As with countless other Christians—including many homemakers—her skills were bottled up, unnoticed and unencouraged in the church.

THE EXPERIENCE OF LOVE INC. shows that if requests for ministry are important, varied, specific and personal, if they are broken up into manageable portions, and if they are accompanied by encouragement, Christ's people will respond. Ministry is like crime. A crime requires a motive, a means and an opportunity. Every act of Christian caring also requires motivation, means and opportunity. Many church members are already motivated and are waiting for someone to provide the means and the opportunity.

Indeed, church members have a hunger for ministry. In Holland, as we demonstrated that we were using people effectively, churches would demand more needs. One church in Holland even complained we were discriminating by not sending enough needy people their way!

And as Christians respond to simple requests to minister, they become sensitized to needs. They notice needs they never saw before. Volunteers then become a source of information about people who need assistance. The pace of ministry picks up.

As I have seen the readiness of Christians to minister, I have glimpsed what the church could be if it were a body of care-*givers* rather than a collection of those who mainly receive ministry. The difference would be like that between an ordinary classroom and the most exciting class I ever took part in. In most classrooms the teacher offers instruction and students listen and absorb.

But some years ago I had the pleasure of leading a different kind of graduate class at the University of Michigan. The subject was "setting up jail and prison libraries.'' I involved each of the students in doing just that in an actual jail or prison setting. As a result they were constantly running into very immediate challenges. Inevitably at every class one of the students would say, "I have a problem to solve. Maybe we could talk about it tonight"—and we would get into a lively discussion of how to handle the difficulty he or she was facing. In two semesters, there wasn't a single evening when I went through my lecture uninterrupted by students wanting to get practical advice about how to do their job better.

Wouldn't it be great, I have often thought, if the church were like that when we got together on Sunday mornings? As I have watched Christians moving into ministry, I have come to believe it could happen.

The Man Who Needed Almost Everything

IF IT HADN'T BEEN for the women's glasses he was wearing, Rob would have looked almost normal. As it was, he seemed in better shape than the other men at the rescue mission. He didn't smell of alcohol, and from the look of his eyes, the program director didn't think he was using drugs.

The Fresno, California, Love Inc. program director, Alan Doswald, was visiting the rescue mission with several other Christians. Rob struck him as a man who might not be too far from the path back into ordinary life.

Alan chatted with Rob for a few minutes. The pressures of two jobs and tremendous stresses at home had overwhelmed him, he learned. Two years ago Rob's personal life had crashed and burned, and he had wandered away from the wreckage into an aimless day-to-day existence, showing up now and then at the rescue mission.

Rob was willing to talk. But his face had a distant, vacant look, and his sentences trailed off inconclusively.

The next time Alan visited the rescue mission, Rob was there. Again the two men talked.

"You could come in off the streets, Rob," Alan told him. "The Lord will help you."

"Yeah, I used to go to church," Rob replied non-committally. "But I stopped a long time ago."

"There's help available," the program director pressed. "I can find a lot of Christians who would help you out. If you ever want help, give me a call. Here's my card with my phone number."

The next day, Rob called. "OK, I'll give it a try. I don't know if I can do it, but I'll give it a try."

Alan began to pray and make phone calls.

The need-analysis procedure ascertained that there were no warrants out for Rob's arrest. His story about dropping out of normal life seemed to prove true. Alan started looking for a place for Rob to stay.

A parishioner of a nearby church who made a living by buying, repairing and reselling apartments was willing to have Rob stay in a place he was fixing up. But when he met Rob, he decided to invite him to stay in his own home.

That was a good beginning, but just a beginning. Rob had nothing but the shabby clothes on his back and a few things jammed in a grocery bag. Love Inc. asked members of a church to donate personal items. Members of another church gave bedding and towels. Two church-operated clothing closets came up with used clothing.

From another church came a man who worked for the department of rehabilitation and was willing to sit down with Rob and talk over his job situation. He helped Rob write out a resume.

Rob contacted an old friend and got a job selling cars. Now he needed good clothes. Two churches chipped in $150 each so he could buy some. So that he could get to work, yet another church bought him a bus pass for a month. And a Christian optometrist fixed him up with a new pair of glasses.

To take care of him after that, someone donated a used car. The car needed some minor repairs, and also something major—a new transmission. From one church a mechanic was found who made the minor repairs free of charge. A mechanic from another church installed a new transmission. Now that he is working, Rob will be able to pay for insurance, and then he will be able to drive the car.

While all of this was happening, a church has been collecting furniture for the day when Rob will be able to get his own place.

Altogether, Christians belonging to eight churches in town have helped Rob get his life together again.

Rob has a long way to go. But he is off to a new start. He has been experiencing reconciliation with God and has been attending church regularly with the family he is staying with. He has also been giving a portion of every paycheck to the rescue mission in appreciation for their help.

HELP IS JUST AROUND THE CORNER

Recently Alan asked Rob what it was that finally motivated him to come in off the streets.

"I decided to give it a try because someone really cared about me," he answered. "That gave me hope."

PART 2

The Quality of Christian Caring

The Most Important Question of All

TONY SAT RESTLESSLY in the visitors' waiting room at the prison. He had been asked to come and see an inmate named Marty. Tony had shown up, but Marty hadn't.

What's the problem? Tony wondered.

After a long wait, Rich, the leader of the group of prison volunteers, came over to him. "I'm sorry," he said. "It looks as if Marty isn't ready to see you tonight. Would you be willing to come back next week?"

The next week Tony came again. Again Marty failed to appear.

I'm wasting my time, Tony thought. A couple of months before, he had felt God's leading to become a prison volunteer. He wanted to put his faith to work. When Love Inc. advertised for Christian men willing to spend some time listening and talking to prison inmates, Tony felt it was something he could do. Now it seemed he had made a mistake. "I'm going to tell Rich that I'm not coming back again," Tony decided.

Rich walked over to where he was sitting. "I'm sorry, Tony," he said. "I know Marty refused to see you last week, and I'm afraid he isn't willing to see you tonight either."

Tony nodded, feeling the disappointment.

"I wonder," Rich continued, "if you would mind trying the telephone this time? It's very important that someone talk with him."

"Yes," Tony replied, "if you want me to."

"Let me tell you about Marty," Rich said. "This fellow had three brothers and sisters and lived with his mother. The mother married some guy who abused her brutally. One day Marty killed his stepfather to protect his mother. His mother and brothers and sisters disowned him. They refuse even to acknowledge that he exists."

Tony had no idea what he could say to Marty, but he picked up the phone. After a minute Marty came on the line.

"Hello, Marty."

There was no response, only breathing.

"Marty," he continued, "my name is Tony. I'd like to talk with you."

Still no response. The silence stretched out uncomfortably long.

Finally Marty spoke. "I'd like to ask one question," he said.

"What's that?"

"Does anybody love me?"

SIX

The Potential:
Doing What Others Can't

CHRISTIANS ARE NOT ONLY demonstrating their willingness to minister to needy neighbors. Through countless acts of generosity they are showing the *quality* of Christian caring. They have answered the question, Are Christians willing to minister? and the question, Can they do more than treat the symptoms of people's needs? As we have seen, the welfare department and other agencies, public and private, provide important services but are unable to affect many of people's basic problems. If the church only gives money or food, it goes no deeper than they do in meeting people's needs. The great discovery of twelve years of Love Inc. is that Christian ministry *can* get beyond immediate physical necessities and bring resources to bear at the level of people's deeper needs.

Living skills. The root cause of many people's need

for material help is their lack of some crucial skill for ordinary life. Many families lack the ability or resources to break the cycle of poverty and welfare on their own. Single parents, welfare families, ex-prisoners on parole, deinstitutionalized mental patients, newly unemployed families, destitute street people, refugees, and many others often need help in acquiring basic lessons in living that most of us take for granted.

A simple example was the mother who made a desperate phone call one night to the church volunteer who had been helping her. "Come quick," she said, "my little girl is sick." When the volunteer arrived, she discovered that the girl was very sick indeed and needed to be taken to a hospital. The mother had given her daughter a handful of pills instead of one pill, because she could not read the label.

A more complex case was that of Karen. After giving birth to a second illegitimate, interracial child, Karen's parents sent her on her way, declaring that they wanted no further contact with her. Karen was able to find public assistance and housing, but she did not know how to take care of her apartment or her two young children. She called Love Inc., and the clearinghouse identified church volunteers to minister to many of her needs. One of these was Mary Jo, who became a caring friend. Mary Jo met with Karen on a regular basis and talked about housekeeping and parenting. She also invited Karen and her children to an ice cream social and other events at her church. Karen became involved at the church and is now a regular participant. Moved by the love that strangers demonstrated toward their daughter, Karen's parents have now been reconciled to her. Karen is especially appreciative of the evidence of God's love in Mary Jo's friendship with her.

What Karen and many other people need are supportive, ongoing relationships with others who can share basic living skills with them. Material assistance by itself enables them to survive but does not offer the tools they need to overcome their problems.

Many social workers recognize the limitations on what they can do through bureaucratic channels and feel frustrated by them. One protective services supervisor wrote Love Inc.: "The battered children and broken families in my care have an urgent message for the church—'Welfare systems can only treat the symptoms of need; they can give food and money, but they can never share the living skills and values required to change lives. That is the role of the church.' "

Love Inc. has developed a program called the Family Support System designed to help individuals who need supportive care to master basic living skills. The program equips caring Christians to minister to individuals or families through an integrated program of outreach and evangelism. The model succeeds where welfare systems fail precisely because it creates a contractual helping relationship between church volunteers and clients. The church volunteers become participants in a helping experience designed to teach basic lessons in living regarding nutrition, employment, child care, budgeting, education, and so on. Clients commit themselves to the goal of achieving independent, productive lives.

This kind of personalized care works. I think of the welfare mother of five boys who established a support system with volunteer families in an area church. She asked those families to help her achieve the ambitious objective of escaping the welfare system within one year. To do that she needed more than food, clothing and other material assistance. She needed caring people who could teach her and her children how to read, how to budget and shop economically, how to gain vocational skills and find jobs, how to prepare nutritious meals, and how to clean up and repair their dwelling. With this kind of help, she was able to pursue her goal.

A Love Inc. office in Michigan received the following letter, acknowledging the helpfulness of the support of church volunteers:

"Dear Love Inc.,

"Thank you so much for helping us financially throughout the year. This June it will be a year we've been on the program. We've gained our confidence again that with strict discipline and a lot of hard work we can do it.

"There were a lot of times we wanted to give up, but with Rita, our budgeter, cheering us on, we kept plugging away and are glad we did. We're not only doing well financially, but our dream of buying a house is coming true.

"We learned a lot in this past year, and a lot we learned the hard way; but we also gave up a lot to achieve our goals.

"We owe a lot and can't thank Love Inc. and the local church enough for helping make our dreams come true.

The discipline we learned throughout this year will stay with us a lifetime.

"P.S. If we can help others in any way at all, please let us know."

Self-esteem. The author of the letter talks about "gaining our confidence again." The church volunteer who helped the family with budgeting shared not only advice about how to handle money, but also confidence that they could do it. She "cheered them on." That kind of support can be crucial. Scratch the surface of many people's lives and you will find the conviction that "I can't succeed." Along with it, you will often find the feeling that "I'm no good; I don't count for anything." Much of the help that state and voluntary agencies provide fails to budge these deep-seated attitudes in the people they try to help. Consequently their helping efforts are water poured on sand.

Lack of self-esteem, in particular, can cripple every attempt a person makes to deal with his problems. A feeling of worthlessness can block every effort to change. I am reminded of Walter, a prisoner serving a life sentence at Attica Prison in New York. He worked with me in a prison education program. As we walked from one part of the prison to another, he would stay a half-step behind. However I varied my pace, Walter always managed to keep the same distance behind. Finally I said, "Would you stop that? You're driving me crazy." He shook his head, as though I were asking the impossible. "When you've been hit over the head time and again by people who demand respect, you learn your place," he said.

Deep-rooted as low self-esteem may be, it is not unreachable. What people need is love and acceptance. These are distinctive gifts that Christian ministry has to offer. Only this will heal many people's pain and unlock their potential to lead a fruitful life.

Contrary to the best intentions of agency personnel, agencies often reinforce the self-esteem problems that needy people have. For someone who has a low sense of self-worth, it can be a crushing experience to pass through the welfare department doors and be greeted with "What's your problem today?"

And not only secular but also Christian outreach sometimes grinds people deeper into problems of low self-esteem. A pastor in Atlanta, Bob Lupton, led a group of Christians in a program to provide toys for poor children at Christmas. Volunteers would box the toys up and take them to people's homes. What they found was that the children would be delighted, but the father would head out the back door, and the mother would try in an embarrassed way to thank them for the toys and apologize for her husband. Happily, in the case of Lupton's group, the care-givers realized their mistake. They saw that their way of being generous hurt the parents' self-respect by showing that someone else had to do for their children what they should have been able to do themselves.

Lupton's group decided to change their approach. They found a storefront and fixed it up as a toy store. Mothers and fathers could come and look things over. The store gave them choices. They were able to purchase toys for pennies on the dollar. This way of doing things was sensitive to the needs of the people being served, above all to their need to keep their self-respect.

When people experience care from Christians who do not make them line up at the door or give them a number, but put an arm around their shoulder and pray with them, a disturbing dynamic is set off inside them. People will come back and share, often in very awkward words, how moved they were to be treated as though they were persons to be valued rather than problems to be solved.

One woman with ten children, married to a disabled husband, had passed through every agency in the county. She came to Love Inc. for some assistance. The program director listened to her story and asked how she personally was doing with all the difficulties she faced. The program director was also candid with her about what could be done. "You have some serious problems," she said. "We will do what we can, but we can't do everything. The most important thing we can do for you right now is to pray for you." And she did.

The woman continued to have many needs, but she was so impressed that she came to the Love Inc. office one day and said, "I'm beginning to think maybe God loves me a little bit. I'm going to accept Christ—and I'm going to do it right here."

"That's wonderful," the program director responded. "But why here?"

"Because you people cared enough to ask how I felt inside," the woman explained. She said that she had seen Christ reflected in the faces of the volunteers at the office.

The subject of self-esteem always brings a little personal image to my mind. When my daughter Emily was little, my wife and I would put her to bed together. When she was all settled, we would go, "One, two, three—yeah, Emily!" There are a lot of people who need to hear the same kind of personal affirmation, expressed in a form suitable for their age and situation.

Personal presence. Deeper than the need for living skills, deeper even than the need for tokens of one's personal worth, is the need to be loved. Without love, there is no motivation to overcome obstacles, no hope that life can ever improve. Without love, there may seem to be no reason to go on living. It is at this most basic level that the distinctiveness of personal Christian ministry shines out most clearly.

Again, those who serve in helping agencies are often painfully aware of the limitations that routines and multiple demands place on their ability to extend the friendship that may be a person's most basic need. Often they would like to extend more personal concern, but simply cannot. The following note was sent to an outreach worker at a church who passed it on to me. It was written in very crude handwriting:

"Dear Mrs. McGaffney,

"Hi, how are you? I thought I'd drop you a few lines and let you know I'm thinking of you. I'm not in the mental hospital anymore. Thanks for the prayers. I don't ever have to go back there. Isn't that great? I thought I'd tell you.

"I miss hearing from you. Can we be pen pals forever? You are always cheering me up. I feel pretty low at times. Being away I feel I haven't got a friend in the world. Nobody writes me or comes to see me. They just pray for me.

"Love, Millie."

The outreach worker said this letter was sent to her one month before this young woman died from an overdose of sleeping pills. "I had never answered Millie's letter—too busy filling out forms in triplicate," the outreach worker wrote. "Not one of my proudest achievements. If some good could be made of this sad occasion by retelling the story, please feel free to do so."

Millie's story echoes the story of Marty, the young convict who asked the question, "Does anybody love me?" Unless a person experiences an affirmative answer to that question, no help with the outward aspects of life will make much difference. An affirmative answer, by contrast, can be the catalyst that makes material assistance really helpful. That was the case with Rob, the man who had been out on the streets for a couple of years in Fresno. It was the expressions of care for him by church volunteers that awakened in him the hope that he might get his life back together again. Without that personal element, all the furniture, job help, eyeglasses and the rest would have done no good at all.

Loneliness does not always lead people to despair. But it does lead many people to bizarre or inappropriate behavior—like the woman who created a family out of pictures she cut out of magazines. As you might expect from its name, Love Inc. offices get some peculiar telephone calls. People have thought the organization is a massage parlor, a sex education clinic or a brothel.

So the staff in one city was not surprised when a refugee who could hardly place one English word after another called one night requesting "a woman for love." It was obvious that this unemployed single father was desperately lonely. Like so many people in our society, he needed a friend.

It is precisely in response to the need for friendship that Christians are best equipped to serve. The ability to be present to another person and express concern is not a professional skill that requires years of instruction. It is a human action that any church member can do in the name of Christ. It usually develops naturally and unobtrusively.

Wendy, for example, was a young single woman who responded to a request to drive Caroline to church every Sunday. Caroline, an elderly woman, was moved into an adult foster care home after her son abandoned her and did not know anyone or have any way of getting to church. Wendy discovered that Caroline always had lots to talk about. She got the impression that Caroline couldn't find anyone at the retirement home that she could talk with freely. Her family had forgotten about her. It seemed that Caroline appreciated the opportunity to talk as much as the ride to church. Wendy enjoyed getting to know her, and after a couple of weeks she asked her if she would like to have brunch at a restaurant after church. Caroline was delighted. Sunday brunch together became a custom for the two women.

Christian caring is open to the possibility that people will move beyond the roles of care-giver and care-receiver and become friends.

A Stop at the Golden Arches

PAUL LIVES NEAR a state prison. A member of his church who works with Love Inc. asked him if he would be willing to do a little driving for wives and children of prison inmates. Many of the women and children arrive in town by bus from the larger cities downstate and need someone to take them the rest of the way to the prison.

Paul agreed. The next Saturday he picked up a young woman named Janice and her little boy and little girl at the bus depot and delivered them to the prison. Several hours later he returned to bring them back to the bus.

Everything went fine, except that Paul was annoyed by the way the two children acted. They were surly when he picked them up in the morning, and twice as bad-tempered and hard to control when he came back in the afternoon.

Paul mentioned this to the contact person at his church. She pointed out that the children's behavior might have something to do with their experience of the day. The bus ride was long and boring, and there was little for them to do at the prison. Also, they probably did not get lunch or dinner, because their mother, after paying the bus fare (forty dollars for herself alone), probably could not afford it.

Well, Paul thought, *that* part of the problem can be taken care of. The following month, he was asked to pick up Janice and the children again. He took them to the prison as before. But this time when he came to bring them back, he suggested that they stop at McDonald's for a bite to eat. Janice accepted his invitation with surprise and relief. When she and the children climbed on the bus late that afternoon, the children were a bit less wild, and certainly more cheerful, than they had been the month before.

SEVEN

Caring: Going the Extra Mile

THE APOSTLE PAUL SAID THERE are no limits to love's trust, hope and perseverance. Church volunteers today put flesh on those words. They reach out to people that no one wants anything to do with, caring creatively, giving beyond the bare minimum.

The men and women that church members volunteer to help are not always clean, cheerful and sweet-smelling. A man who has been living on the streets is not as nice to be around as a man who showered at the racquet club on his way to work. A couple who are in danger of losing custody of their children because of incompetence and neglect may need someone to help them clean the roaches out of the baby's crib and launder a pile of dirty diapers. Ministry to the needy means meeting Jesus in all His distressing disguises.

In one city after another, Christians have risen to the

challenge. A typical story comes from Alaska. Sarah wanted someone to do chores in her home one day a week. She had been deserted by her husband and was in poor health. As she talked on the phone with the local program director, she sounded very bitter.

Sarah had already received help from several agencies. When the program director spoke with them, she got the same story from each: Sarah was discouraging to work with; she complained all the time; nothing was ever right. She dragged everyone down into her gloom. None of the agencies would continue working with her.

The program director did not expect the churches to meet Sarah's need. But she did call one church, making sure to give the contact person the same information the agencies had given her. She was surprised, the next week, when the church had a volunteer to help Sarah.

The volunteer did some chores for Sarah and spent time visiting with her. She did indeed find Sarah impossible to please. After several weeks the volunteer decided that Sarah was more than she could handle, but she did not give up. She went back to her church contact person and got three more volunteers to work with her.

Twice a week a pair of them now visit Sarah together. They find it easier to work with Sarah when they have each other's support. And they have found that Sarah needs the more frequent contact. They have been doing this and praying for her regularly for six months.

There are no major changes in Sarah's behavior. She may be a little less bitter, and perhaps her smiles come more frequently. But she still complains, and it is difficult to remain joyful around her.

The program director recently asked the church contact person whether the volunteers wanted to continue the helping relationship with Sarah. "Definitely!" she said. "If our people don't love her, who will?"

Paul was perhaps even harder to love. A middle-aged Michigan man, he has been in and out of prison several times. A couple of years ago Paul found himself in trouble yet again. Convicted of minor crimes committed while in an alcoholic stupor, he was incarcerated in a county jail. When he was released, he hitchhiked to his only friend in the area—a young woman who lived ninety miles away. The trip took him nearly the entire day. When he got to her apartment, she told him in no uncertain terms that she did not want him back in her life and slammed the door in his face. No amount of pleading could persuade her to change her mind.

After several days of seeking assistance, Paul found an abandoned farmyard and holed up in the corn crib.

For the first time in his life, Paul despaired. Also for the first time, he turned to God. Paul offered him a grim deal. "God," he prayed, "I will go to church just once. Then I will kill myself."

The next Sunday a member of a local church was driving through town on his way to worship and noticed Paul. On an impulse, he stopped and asked Paul if he needed a ride. After the two men talked for a few minutes, he invited Paul to come to church with him.

For an hour, Paul—a big, hawk-like man, dirty, smelly, missing most of his teeth—sat through a church service in the middle of a very proper congregation. As he sat there, his thoughts were on his plan to go back to the farmyard after church and kill himself.

God inspired a significant number of people to come up to Paul after the service and express a concern for him. Paul decided to suspend his plans for self-destruction. Over the next few days they found a place for him to live and a job. It became apparent that Paul was inclined to drink heavily, so they provided alternative activities for him every night. They invited him into their homes and lives. Some forty members helped in one way or another.

Several months later, Paul was baptized. After the ceremony he told about his determination to kill himself, and the totally unexpected way that God had used the people in the church to intervene in his life. "You shared something with me," he said, "that I had never experienced before: love." After Paul spoke, the pastor wrapped his arms around him, and the church erupted in praise.

Paul still has problems. He is having trouble with alcohol, and the church has helped him get into an alcoholism treatment program. He keeps pledging his desire to minister to people in need, but still has too many needs himself. But the other church members are sticking with him. They are not put off by him.

Christian caring not only reaches out to people we would not ordinarily care to be with. It also offers help that goes beyond the mere basics. It means noticing needs and taking the initiative to meet them. Here, for example, is a thank-you letter written to a Love Inc.

office by a woman who got more help than she bargained for:

"A total hip replacement plus a fracture of my femur during surgery had left me unable to take care of myself. I was in a cast and was confined to a wheelchair.

"A friend of mine belonged to a church which is participating in Love Inc. My friend went to the Love Inc. office, met with the program director and told of my situation and asked what services were available. The next day the director visited my home, described Love Inc., asked me what I needed to maintain an independent life-style, and began to put the Love wheels in motion.

"My limitations during the early recovery were such that just getting to the bathroom was a major and painful production. I know that I would not have fed myself properly had I been left to fend for myself.

"Within the next twenty-four hours I received calls from people who didn't ask what I needed but told me what they were going to do. Nancy sensed my reluctance to ask for help. Bonnie came and took my laundry and continued to do it for a while, and she brought groceries as I needed them. Sharon arrived with her husband and son, who mowed the yard while she visited. A beautiful lady named Opal brought me wonderful home-cooked meals as often as four times a week. I received phone calls and visits every day until many weeks had passed.

"Nancy, recognizing my depression and discomfort with just sitting every day—I am a working lady who needs to be involved with people and life—introduced me to a new handicraft, providing me with all the materials to complete a number of projects. She also drove me the 120 miles each way in her car, with her gas, to see my surgeon for checkups and eventually the removal of the cast. I was given money to help with my utilities by the Episcopal church women, all of whom are involved with Love Inc. in some way. (My sick pay had soon run out.)

"Helen lent me a small table to keep needed objects close at hand, and Nancy brought over an extension lamp so that I could see better. Sue, a doctor's wife, came over and cleaned my house. I received cards of cheer and get-well wishes, and other members continued to call and visit.

"I am still on crutches, but for the most part I can do things for myself now. But the true meaning of Christianity, which was shown me by the Love people, gave me the truest sense of God's love at work—not by words but by action. I am a relative newcomer to this area and cannot imagine how I would have managed without the care provided me. Love people literally saw me through. Thank you!"

When a person in need intersects with a caring Christian, God is revealed in the special kindness and attention to detail that says, "You are special. You are important." Often a little service that is unnecessary from a utilitarian standpoint sends a powerful signal of God's love. Consider these examples:

• Funeral parlors in one town regularly donate sprays of flowers to a nursing home. But the characteristically funereal fans of gladiolas and other flowers would be a sardonic bit of cheer for the elderly people, some of whom may already be contemplating their approaching death. So Margie takes the time to cut the flower arrangements apart and regroups the flowers in new combinations.

• A little girl with cancer is having chemotherapy. She is tolerating the therapy reasonably well, except for the fact that her hair is falling out. Every morning she gets up and looks sadly in the mirror at the bald spots. Children at school make fun of the bandana she has been wearing. Through Love Inc., a group of Christians chip in to buy her a wig.

• A young blind couple have a baby. They call Love Inc. to ask if there is anyone who could help them learn how to take care of their little boy. Love Inc. locates a nurse, who comes and helps them master the procedures of bathing and diapering the baby. The volunteer's greatest thrill, however, is describing the baby's appearance to the parents, giving them the chance to get better acquainted with their own child.

And here, as further testimony to generosity going beyond what is strictly needed, is a letter from a young woman who received help from church volunteers through a Love Inc. clearinghouse in Michigan:

"When the folks at Love Inc. met me, I was on welfare, in need of housing, and felt like Raggedy Ann. My family was in far-off California, unable to help. But the Lord works in mysterious and wondrous ways. I found Love.

"As I was qualifying for job training, the volunteers at Love found me housing, even with my cherished pet dog, and helped me get on my feet. I qualified for college, and during my first semester as a vision-impaired student a volunteer helped me by taping my books. They helped me with transportation and moral support when my health failed me, and countless loving little miracles.

"I had come so far in the past year and a half. I am an honors student at the college, have two wonderful part-time campus jobs, and am on my way. But I faltered at having to spend another Christmas alone. My friends all went home or had obligations, and I felt even worse that I couldn't emotionally handle the prospect of being by myself.

"I confided in Jenny that I was determined to handle this. But she and Love decided that I should not. Christmas Eve day she called to tell me I was going home to California—Christmas Day, with the last ticket available. All the arrangements had been made. A volunteer got up at 4:00 a.m. Christmas Day to drive me to the airport. Several hours later I got to hug and kiss my mom for the first time in four years.

"And the trip did more than just that. It gave me a new sense of self-worth and new strength to meet the challenge that lies ahead."

A thank-you like that will keep you going for a long time.

"Would You Like to See My Children?"

IN A MICHIGAN CITY, Love Inc. was asked to find volunteers to transport people without families to a free Thanksgiving dinner at a local steakhouse. On Thanksgiving Day volunteers picked up people not only at retirement and nursing homes but also under bridges and viaducts and from abandoned buildings.

Lea picked up one woman at an adult foster care home. The woman was quite old and had a severe speech impediment. She got in the car with Lea and talked nonstop. It was obvious she had not talked to anyone in a long time.

After about ten minutes the woman said to Lea, "May I show you some pictures of my children?"

"Sure," Lea answered.

The woman took out her wallet, which was falling apart, and flipped through pictures. With each picture there was a story. This child had done such and such when she was young; that child had liked potato chips; this boy had liked walking in the mud—picture after picture after picture.

Soon Lea was choking back the tears. All the pictures were cut out of magazines and newspapers. The old woman had created a family out of fantasies, from a need to have people close to her.

EIGHT

The Heart: Ministering With Christ

C HRIST HIMSELF PLAYS THE central role in Christian caring. Ultimately, this gives Christian ministry its distinctive character. Behind the efforts of church members to help their neighbors there is more than human compassion, and certainly more than the guilt that often motivates outreach to the needy. Behind Christian ministry is Jesus Christ Himself. Care for the needy today, like the Samaritan's care for the roadside victim in the parable told long ago, was Christ's idea before it became ours.

Indeed, if we wish to see God, we should look at the point where a caring Christian intersects with a person in need. The simple, friendly service of Christian people to the needy is one of the chief places where God manifests Himself in this world. As Kathleen Busse, the director of Love Inc. in Chicago's western suburbs, says simply, "As we express love for others, we see the reality of God's love among us."

Sometimes it is those who are served who see Him most clearly. A woman in California who received furniture through arrangements made by Love Inc. said to the local program director, "I feel as if the shadow of God is over me." It was clear to her that the help she received came not only from the people who brought it, but also from Christ who inspired them to give.

Sometimes Christian caring, by its generosity, opens the way for a person to recognize Christ for the first time. This happened to Cheryl, a single mother in Alaska. She was due to have a baby in two-and-a-half weeks and asked Love Inc. for transportation to a doctor's appointment. Love Inc. called a church in her neighborhood, and the contact person found a volunteer to drive her.

The volunteer discovered that Cheryl faced a number of difficulties. She had serious medical problems, but the doctor would not see her again without being paid. The cheap room in which she and her young son lived had no furniture and was unhealthy.

Love Inc. asked the church if they would develop a team of people who could address these problems, and they did. One volunteer helped Cheryl apply for low-income housing. When she was accepted, a group of volunteers helped her move. A payment agreement was reached with the doctor's office, so that she could continue getting medical assistance. A volunteer helped her set up a budget and taught her money-management skills. Still another volunteer tutored her in a childbirth program and stayed with her in the hospital when she had her baby.

Some weeks later, when Cheryl was being driven to the doctor, she turned to the volunteer and asked, "Why are you people doing all this for me?" The volunteer then had the opportunity to tell her what Christ has done to forgive our sins and make our lives new, and to give us His love to share with others.

A poignant example of Christian caring opening the way for Christ to make Himself known involved another single mother. She was a shut-in who called Love Inc. asking if they could find anyone to bring some food to her apartment. When a church volunteer placed the groceries on her table, the woman was nearly in tears.

"Thank you so much," she said. "You'll never know what this food means to me and my children."

"Don't thank me," the volunteer replied. "Thank Jesus. We are doing it in His name."

The woman paused before responding. "Would you thank Him for me?" she said. "I don't know who He is."

Some are caught totally unawares by the generosity of Christian caring—almost as if Christ had come along as the Gospels describe Him, walking along the roadside and unexpectedly healing someone who was blind or crippled. Steve Reid, program director in Barry County, Michigan, reports that a church involved in the program has designed a second follow-up procedure. They do something no agency would ever do: they call the client to see if he still has a need! If he does, they ask whether they can pray with him, and they share Jesus Christ. People are amazed that anyone cares intensely enough to call. Last year twenty people accepted Christ as a result of this ministry.

There is no way to measure the importance of caring that makes Christ known. Regardless of the outcome, the opportunity to speak the gospel is priceless. This was brought home to some volunteers in a small town, as the program director later explained:

"Bill came to Love Inc. late Tuesday morning to ask for food. A Love Inc. volunteer interviewed him, could sense Bill's genuine need and was thankful for the opportunity to refer him to a church food bank not far from the Love Inc. office.

"The food bank volunteer felt compelled to talk to Bill about Jesus. It was as if the Spirit would not let her avoid speaking to this young man of Jesus' love. The young man listened patiently to her witness before leaving the food bank at 2:00 p.m. with the food and God's blessing.

"That night at 7 p.m. Bill was struck and killed by a truck. No one knows if the young man committed his life to Christ that day. We do know that the volunteer was able to share her witness with this fellow because her church was involved in ministry, giving her the opportunity to respond to his physical and spiritual needs."

BECAUSE CHRIST IS AT THE center of Christian caring, Love Inc. seeks to be openly identified with Him. We avoid being pushy or offensive about the gospel, but we want to wear the name of Christ clearly, so that people can see the ultimate source of the help they receive.

For this reason we maintain Love Inc.'s explicit Christian label. "Love Inc." captures the purpose of the organization—to show love—and the method—to activate the body of Christ ("incorporated" has to do with being a body). Through no efforts of our own, the "Inc." has also come to take on a further meaning among those who staff the affiliates around the country: "In the name of Christ." As staff workers in various parts of the country have affirmed this interpretation, I have sensed the Spirit of God clarifying the purpose of our organization.

There have been challenges to our policy of explicit Christian ministry. I was invited to make a presentation about Love Inc. in a city in the South. Afterward a prominent pastor stood up and indicated total support for the Love Inc. ministry model. But he expressed his desire to develop an interfaith clearinghouse in the area and wondered if we would be willing to delete the name of Christ from our materials. I explained to him that that would cut the heart out of the ministry.

In a city in the West, an agency representative attempted to use our materials to develop an unauthorized Love Inc. program with a different name. She called pastors together and presented her plan. A Presbyterian minister was the first to question her. He inquired whether she was trying to set up a Love Inc. program. She replied that her plan was "loosely based on the Love Inc. model—but without the Christian component." The minister responded that she did not understand that when she took Christ out of the ministry, there could be no ministry.

(Sometimes it is not our Christian label but the word "love" in our title that gives people problems. The Fairbanks, Alaska, Love Inc. set up shop in a room in the Polaris Hotel, a rendezvous for illicit sex. The local staff insisted that in that environment they needed a different name to avoid misunderstandings. But after a few months of straightening out misunderstandings, they reported that they were glad they had kept "love" in their name, because they saw God redeeming it by showing its true meaning.)

RECOGNIZING THAT CHRISTIAN caring originates with Christ and is expressed through His church, Love Inc. clearinghouses have adopted the policy of relying entirely on church and private donations. We refuse to accept government funding. The ministry of Love Inc. attempts to stir up the church of Christ to show the love of Christ. If Love Inc. were to become a conduit for government funds, it would defeat this purpose.

In at least one instance, a local Love Inc. office has had to act decisively to maintain its explicitly Christian character in the face of the "threat" of government support. Alaska state senator Paul Fischer learned of Love Inc. in the Kenai Peninsula and proposed state funding for it without consulting with the chairwoman or program director. The Love Inc. office there politely refused. The president gave this explanation in the local newspaper:

"Senator Paul Fischer's basic assessment is correct. The Love Inc. community clearinghouse 'provides no direct services and does not duplicate existing helping services. It screens needs and organizes churches to work with agencies in meeting individual, family and project needs.' We do so without regard to a person's religious beliefs or church affiliation.

"As a grassroots organization we seek to involve the Christian community in taking care of requests for help not met by state or local agencies or other charities. Our bylaws specifically mandate that the members of our corporation are to be participating local churches with the purpose of showing the love of Christ by meeting individual or community needs.

"Sen. Fischer endorsed our efforts as a clearinghouse by making a request for state funding. We thank him for his endorsement, but we cannot accept state funds because of our stated purpose and bylaws."

It may be that those who are most keenly appreciative of the opportunity for ministry rendered explicitly in the name of Christ are Christians who work for secular helping agencies. They see the supreme importance of communicating the love of Christ but are restricted in their ability to do so. A human services worker in Oregon wrote:

"Our agency is doing a good work and has provided relief and support for a lot of people. But the greatest weakness of our program, as I see it, is an inability to make a lasting impact on people's lives. We are merely dealing with symptoms, and the root causes continue to go untouched. The cycle of dependency our families are caught in is almost impossible to break. Two things I see that are sorely lacking or nonexistent in our program are (1) a lack of significant and meaningful relationships between the helper and client (this varies from person to person), and (2) the freedom to share the gospel of Jesus Christ. I believe these two things go hand in hand, and therein lies an ability to make a significant impact on people's lives. That's why I like Love Inc."

A Minnesota woman who was a welfare client and later became a welfare caseworker drew a similar lesson about the value of explicitly Christian ministry:

"What is so frustrating to me is that most all of these people need to know God's healing love. I can't talk about Jesus to them as part of my job. Another thing they need is some person in their life who cares. There generally isn't anyone, just agencies.

"Thank you so much, Love Inc., for being. Knowing the welfare system as we do, my husband and I have felt for a long time that the body of Christ should be doing this, not some government agency. You can't legislate love, compassion and discernment."

IN CHRISTIAN MINISTRY we are in a working relationship with Christ. He gives directions. We rely on Him. More than good ideas are involved. Christ Himself works out His plans.

For me, one of the most impressive demonstrations of this has been the variety of people who have testified that the Lord gave them a vision for Love Inc. This has happened on at least four occasions:

• In Milwaukee when I gave a presentation on Love Inc. one woman listened intently but said nothing in the discussion. Afterward she came up to me and told me she had been deeply moved by my talk. She explained that shortly before he died, her husband had called her into the bedroom and told her that God had given him a vision for a Christian clearinghouse that should be called Love Inc. Her husband showed her a chart of how the organization should be set up—a chart that matched the one I had used in my presentation.

• In Huntington, Indiana, I met a woman who told me that God had given her a vision for meeting needs like that of Love Inc., but He had told her to wait. From my presentation she saw that Love Inc. fulfilled the vision the Lord had given her. She later became chairwoman of the Love Inc. board of directors in Huntington.

• In Woodland, Washington, a woman recounted a similar story. She told me that two years earlier the Lord had given her a vision for a system like Love Inc. but had told her to wait. When she read an article about Love Inc., she was convinced it was the right moment. Her sense of timing seemed to be confirmed by the fact that all the pastors in the community joined the planning committee.

• In Denver a man said that, even before he had heard of Love Inc., God had shown him a way of dividing the city into zones around churches. When I sketched two ways of zoning for Love Inc. in Denver, he identified one of them as the arrangement God had shown him. When Love Inc. was launched in Denver, it began with that zoning arrangement.

In these ways, through shared awareness, I have heard God saying, "Virgil, this isn't your ministry; it's My ministry and the church's ministry."

Because it is Christ's ministry, the men and women who share in it do so in response to His call. Many who are involved, from church volunteers to program directors, can tell how they recognized His call.

A retired couple in Lansing, Michigan, wanted to offer their time to help meet needs. They heard about Love Inc. and went to talk with the program director, Mary Ann Harkema. "We want to do something," they told her. "We want to share, to witness—but we don't know what to do."

While they were talking, a call came in. Mary Ann took the call and talked awhile. When she hung up the phone, she said to the couple, "Let me tell you about this girl. We get a lot like her. She is a single mother; she is lonely; she has lots of needs, and she doesn't even understand her own needs. We really should have someone who could go to the home and visit the family, help her understand her needs and then develop a relationship."

"We could do that," the couple said.

They started there and are now serving twelve single mothers. Through that phone call they heard Christ's call. Their response became the springboard to a whole new opportunity to care. Already they are affecting the lives of several women and children. Who knows how many others may be touched in the future?

Sometimes Christ's call comes clearly to a person, but the path for responding takes a twist or two. Jenny Forner was a high-energy businesswoman who ran her own catering and bridal businesses and helped her husband run his heating and refrigeration business in

Allendale, Michigan. Every fall, like thousands of other Michigan residents, the two of them would take off for a few days to go deer hunting. While her husband crouched in a blind for hours, waiting for a deer to come along, Jenny would go out and sit somewhere else in the woods and meditate. One day as she was praying and thinking, she heard the Lord ask her, "Jenny, what are you doing for Me?" As she pondered the question, her answer was, "Not nearly as much as I want to."

When she got back to town she went to her church board and said, "I'm available to do whatever you want me to do, six hours a week." The elders could not remember anyone ever making such an offer. They asked her to give them a little time to think it over.

Weeks went by, and the board never got back to her. So Jenny decided to take matters into her own hands. She took some office partitions from her business, put them in a pickup truck and drove them over to the church. She set up a workplace for herself and began coming in two mornings a week, looking for whatever needed to be done. No one gave her much of anything to do, so she developed some projects of her own. She wrote letters of encouragement to missionaries that the church helped to sponsor and thank-you notes to people who taught in Sunday school.

One day a visiting church official walked through the area and demanded to know what she was doing. "Are you angling for a place on the church board?" he asked.

Frustrated and rejected, Jenny cleared out her partitions and went home. She had been sure the Lord was calling her to serve Him, and she wanted to respond.

But it seemed impossible. For months she felt angry and depressed.

Then, through a counselor she was seeing, Jenny heard about Love Inc. As she looked into it, she became convinced that this was where God was calling her to serve. In the years since then, she has cut back her time in her own businesses and has become the program director of Love Inc. in the Allendale, Michigan, area.

When Christ inspires men and women to minister in His name, He sustains them in the work He calls them to do. Learning to rely on Him is one of the challenges of Christian caring. It is a lesson that many of us learn only with difficulty. But the unpredictable demands of the work make it a lesson that we can hardly avoid.

Kathleen Busse, director of Love Inc. in Chicago's west suburbs, observes that volunteers who staff the office "come here wanting to do so much, God love them. But many of them come from areas of life—at home or in business—where they're in control. Here they're not in control. You don't know who's going to call. And when people call, you're not in control of any resources. God has to bring the resources. That's hard to come to terms with. But after a while they learn that there is always the point where you have to let go and trust God. If we recognize our limitations, we will realize that in our weakness is His strength."

On the wall in the Love Inc. office hangs a large picture of Jesus walking on the Sea of Galilee to the disciples in the boat, with Peter venturing out toward Him. When the staff reaches the end of their capabilities and needs to be reminded to trust in Christ, Kathleen will point to the picture and say, "I hear the sloshing, but I haven't got any water in my shoes yet!" It is a marvelous way of expressing the fact that Christ Himself is at the heart of Christian caring.

Least Likely to Succeed

WHEN NEIL, A YOUNG California man, was released from prison, he returned to his wife and made the rounds of local churches looking for help. After a few weeks he found work and began to attend one church regularly. But he was a long way from being able to meet all his own needs.

Love Inc. first heard from Neil when his car broke down and he could not afford to repair it. The clearinghouse found a mechanic from his own church to fix his car. Later Neil called asking for food, and Love Inc. located a church volunteer to work out a budget with him. Then he called needing dental work. He had a large cavity and was in constant pain and was self-medicating with his wife's pain medication. He knew he must get his tooth fixed and get a legal prescription for medication before an upcoming meeting with his parole officer.

After consulting with his church, Love Inc. found him a dentist to take care of his tooth and provide the prescription.

After his parole meeting, Neil's parole officer called the people at the church who had been working with him. The officer shared with them how he had noticed a measurable change in his client's attitude. "I confess," the parole officer said, "that I never thought this guy could make it. But I'm glad to see that he is."

NINE

The Results: Exceeding Expectations

CHRISTIAN CARING MINISTERS not just to needs but to persons. Thus it can have an impact that goes beyond alleviating a person's immediate distress. Love is a creative power. Christian ministry in Christ's love can unleash hidden potentialities within a person. It can enable a person not only to cope with problems but to surmount them.

This is the case with Dorothy, who found in the help of church volunteers the strength to open a new chapter in her life after Mike deserted her. It is the case with Ace, the motorcycle gang member who found the help he needed to settle down and take hold of the responsibilities of fatherhood. It is the case with Joanne, who, even on her tight budget, has begun to reach out to others by donating baby formula and diapers to another family in need. It is the case with Neil, who is drawing on the help of many people to overcome his parole officer's prediction of "unlikely to make it."

One of the most striking effects of Christian caring is that it gives people the freedom and desire to become helpers themselves. Sometimes the response is a simple gesture of gratitude. A woman appears at the door of a food bank with a bag of groceries and explains that, while she is still on welfare, she wants to give some food "in case there are others who could use it." Another woman, who has just been delivered some furniture by church volunteers, asks one of the volunteers if he would like to have a child's wading pool for his own children.

In other cases, the response is more substantial. A couple in Michigan was helped through Love Inc. when their son was murdered in another state and they needed money to travel to the funeral. When they returned, they informed Love Inc. that they would repay the money by providing used furniture from their small auction service whenever the program had that need. (Little did they know that the program had been trying to find a source of furniture for occasional needs.)

A young woman who was an abusive mother accepted the offer of a church volunteer to be her friend and advisor. The volunteer, who had successfully raised several children, shared parenting skills and love with her. The young woman remarried and was able to establish a stable family environment. Later she called Love Inc. to express her appreciation for the volunteer and to offer to become herself a caring friend for an abusive mother.

And change works both ways in Christian caring. Sometimes the one helping is the more deeply affected.

Tim, who worked in a Denver service station, was unhappy with his job and spent a lot of time thinking about his future. The Love Inc. contact person in his church called him one evening and asked if he could help the Figueroa family. Chico Figueroa had been out of work for a long time. Now he was employed again, but the car that he relied on to get to work had quit. Could Tim take a look at it?

"Well, it's not what I was planning to do tonight," Tim replied, although he did not have anything planned. "I guess I'll go over and check it out."

While Tim diagnosed the problem, he got into a conversation with Chico. He came back the next day with new parts, and they had another long talk. When the car was fixed, Chico invited him to dinner. After that, Tim invited Chico and his family to visit the church.

The next time Tim saw the contact person at church, he told her, "I felt useless and depressed before. But helping the Figueroa family has given me new hope. I can't remember being happier."

IF THE EFFECTS OF CHRISTIAN caring exceed ordinary expectations in terms of personal change, they also exceed the usual effects of agency care on the very utilitarian scale of cost effectiveness. Inspired by Christ, believers are often highly motivated, to the point of making real sacrifices. They can also tap the skills and material resources of church members. Therefore they often achieve a level of efficiency that is impossible elsewhere.

For example, after working together in the Love Inc. network for a few years, twenty-six churches in Holland, Michigan, knew enough about local needs to see the usefulness of a shelter for women who are victims of domestic violence. They have operated such a shelter now for ten years. The churches contribute a combined total of $12,000 a year to the home, and they provide house parents and over fifty volunteers to run it. A comparable shelter home financed by tax dollars would exceed $200,000 a year.

A church in Holland developed a day-care treatment program for mentally ill adults. Ten volunteers met twice a month with mentally ill residents of adult foster care homes. Their purpose was simple yet dramatic: to equip these people for independent living. Several people achieved the goal. The budget for this project was less than ten dollars a month.

Churches in one community provided, at no cost, a furniture service that was offered by a national agency for $30,000 a year.

A number of Love Inc. clearinghouses are able to operate on budgets of less than $5,000 a year, because volunteer church members, not the clearinghouse staffs, provide the services.

A token of agency representatives' appreciation of the cost effectiveness of Christian ministry is this letter from a district manager of the department of social services in Michigan to Marvin Baker, Love Inc. program director in Muskegon County:

"Thank you so much for the financial assistance recently extended to Mr. Crane. The efforts put forth by Love Inc. [in paying his sixty-three-dollar automobile repair bill] enabled Mr. Crane to keep his employment, as well as negating the necessity of opening up a public assistance case for him. That savings alone is approximately $1,200 per month plus medical coverage.''

If one considers the potential dollar value of church services within a typical community, the totals are awesome. Love Inc. made the following estimate of the resources in one Michigan city:

churches	150
church members (150 per church)	22,500
volunteer hours per year	
(1 per week per member)	1,170,000
donations per year	
($1 per week per member)	$1,170,000
value of volunteer services per year	
(time at $10 per hour plus donations)	$12,870,000

The critical figure is not the total dollar value or even the number of churches. The totals for ten churches ($858,000), five churches ($429,000) and even one church ($85,000) are impressive. Of far greater significance is the fact that these staggering totals are comprised primarily of volunteer services that are readily available within all churches—teachers and tutors, budget planners, home economists, plumbers, carpenters, electricians, successful parents and grandparents, drivers, companions, and so on.

While such utilitarian measures are eye-opening, we must not lose sight of the essential values of Christian caring, which have to do more with matters of the heart than with matters of the pocketbook. A church volunteer ministering in a way that has no cash value may yet be sharing the love of Christ. Indeed, sometimes in God's eyes the value of Christian caring does not lie in its effectiveness. A service that fails to have any result may be exceedingly worthwhile. One such service asked church volunteers to knit mittens for residents of an adult foster-care home. A woman whose hands were badly misshapen by arthritis wanted so much to help that she managed to produce a pair of mittens—which were as misshapen as her own hands. But surely the terrible pain she endured in making those useless mittens counted for something in God's eyes.

BEFORE LEAVING THE SUBJECT of expectations it is worth pointing out that the expectations of the person who ministers may be different from those of the person who receives the ministry. What seems insignificant or unsuccessful to the care-giver may seem valuable to the recipient. Judging by our own standards, we may feel that the people we are caring for are making little progress and be tempted to give up. But we may have no idea how important our friendship and support may be in the eyes of the person we are helping.

In one case church volunteers were helping a single mother with two children. The mother's primary need was for budget planning. The daughter needed positive role models. The son simply needed to know that somebody cared about him. Love Inc. helped to make the connections.

154

One day the church representative called the program director and said, "I just don't think this is working. Maybe we should just discontinue the relationship."

So the program director said, "Let's all meet."

The program director, the church representative and the mother got together, and the church representative asked, "Would we be doing you a favor if we just dropped this whole arrangement?"

The woman burst into tears. "Don't you realize what's happening?" she said. "For the first time in my life our finances are under control; they don't control us. My daughter goes out bowling or something else once a week with a woman who is teaching her how to dress and take care of herself. My little boy is involved in youth activities at the church and has a big brother...."

The church representative suddenly came face to face with the fact that he had imposed his expectations on that family. If they did not make progress at his speed, on his timetable, the arrangement seemed not to be working. But from the woman's perspective, it was the most fantastic thing that had happened to her.

Shall We Hug?

CHRISSIE, the five-year-old girl next door, comes from a broken home with a shadowy legacy of violence. She spends the greater part of every day playing with my two daughters.

Chrissie has a hygiene problem. If she has been playing indoors at my house, especially in the winter, I notice the odor as soon as I arrive.

Every afternoon when I get home I toss my girls in the air, kiss them and tell them I love them. For a long time Chrissie studied this ritual from a distance. Day after day I felt her eyes on me as I greeted my girls.

One day as Chrissie and my daughters were walking to the swings in the backyard, I heard her say, "I like it when your dad kisses you."

A few days later she said to me very seriously, "You always hug your daughters and kiss your wife when

157

you get home.''

About a week after that when I arrived home one afternoon, I thought the moment had come. After giving my own girls hugs and kisses, I got on my knees, opened my arms and asked Chrissie, ''May I give you a hug?''

I could almost see the confused memories crossing her face. After a minute, she came to me, and I embraced her.

In a small but significant way, I have had an impact on Chrissie's life. In order to do it, it did not matter whether I was the director of Love Inc. or the king of Siam. What mattered was that I had convinced her of my authenticity as a father. Authenticity had created the opportunity for ministry.

PART 3

Love Inc.
Today and Tomorrow

A New Furnace and a New Outlook on Life

DIANA HUCKABA, a single mother in her mid-thirties, was in almost constant pain. A childhood spinal defect, worsened by an auto accident, kept her in bed all day. From her bed she somehow managed to care for her children. As she struggled through each day, the worst part was that nobody seemed to care. Diana seemed to be closed off in the circle of her problems. To crown it all, in the middle of a Michigan winter, her furnace broke down.

"I had no money and didn't know where to turn," Diana says now. "But as it turned out, that furnace breaking was the turning point in my life."

When Diana called a local heating company, the woman she spoke to put her in touch with Love Inc. The Love Inc. program director counseled with her regarding her physical and emotional needs and referred her case to a little-known government program which was able to help her. Before she knew it, she had a new furnace.

Soon after, she had a new outlook on life. Experiencing a Christian's personal concern had a powerful impact on her. "Since getting involved in the program, the entire community has reached out to embrace me. Love Inc. has given me back my dignity," Diana says.

With the encouragement of new Christian friends, Diana grew confident that she could overcome the challenges she faced. Her health has improved. Now she shares with others the love that she has found herself. On days when she is feeling up to it, Diana volunteers at Love Inc. "My entire life has changed," she says. She has left isolation and abandonment behind and has found the freedom to serve.

TEN

Milestones Passed,
Lessons Learned

FROM HOLLAND, MICHIGAN, in 1976, Love Inc. has spread across the country. The success of the clearinghouse model in city after city, in all regions of the country, has demonstrated the willingness of church members to minister.

After Holland, the next city to have a Love Inc. clearinghouse was Flint, Michigan, in 1981. In the early 1980s Flint stood as the symbol of the wrenching readjustment of the American economy to declining industrial competitiveness. A heavily auto-manufacturing-dependent city since the 1930s, Flint's unemployment rate climbed to a level not seen since the Great Depression (twenty-seven percent in 1981), and physical hunger—usually considered a Third-World scourge—appeared as a measurable problem. In that year five Flint pastors decided to use the Love Inc. model to bring church resources to bear on this massive crisis. The program initially developed in the two-square-mile area of greatest need. It quickly grew to encompass the entire city and now the entire county.

In the following year, again at the initiative of local pastors, a Love Inc. clearinghouse began taking calls in Hammond, Indiana. In 1987 we established a Love Inc. office in Denver, testing the model in a major metropolitan area.

During the 1980s various Christian agencies in various cities were examining their approach to ministry and reaching the same conclusion that led to the launching of Love Inc. in Holland. In Fresno, California; Bradenton, Florida; Marietta, Georgia; and Cedar Rapids, Iowa, agencies similar to Holland's Good Samaritan Center concluded that they were not fulfilling their God-given mission of involving church members in ministry. On the basis of their independent evaluations, they initiated efforts to open a Love Inc. clearinghouse in their cities.

National publicity spurred inquiries from across the country. The leading evangelical magazine, *Christianity Today*, reported on the Holland, Michigan, operation in the fall of 1981. Syndicated columnist Michael McManus described us in a column in 1984.

By 1988, fifty-six clearinghouses were operating in the United States. They were drawing 1,500 churches into partnership in ministry and were answering 12,000 new requests each month. Regional training centers in Fresno and Chicago were preparing new program directors. In the first half of 1988, we received some 250 requests for information from thirty-eight states and four foreign countries—all with virtually no marketing. More than eighty percent of the inquiries came from lay people.

Like most Christian ministries, Love Inc. has constantly operated on the financial edge. One particularly critical moment occurred in 1985. We faced the necessity of borrowing a third time to keep the organization afloat. My wife, Kathy, and I decided that we would ask the Lord for an indication of His will. I felt that the Spirit of God fixed the sum of $50,000 in my mind. We prayed and asked God to supply that amount within a week if He wanted us to carry on. That would involve a gift three times larger than any we had received before. On the morning of the seventh day I received a phone call from a man I had never met who informed me that a foundation had decided to grant Love Inc. $120,000, to be given in three annual installments of $50,000, $40,000 and $30,000. God had shown us what He wanted us to do!

The most recent chapter in Love Inc.'s growth is the program's adoption by World Vision, a major evangelical relief organization. World Vision, as its title indicates, serves needy people around the world. But the organization channels two percent of its $120-million annual budget to domestic needs. The organization's policy is to work in or through churches, rather than setting up competing agencies. In 1986 the fit between World Vision's policy and the Love Inc. approach of helping churches to mobilize their members for ministry became apparent. In 1987 our two organizations formed a partnership, and in 1988 the relationship advanced from cooperation to unification. Love Inc. became a division of World Vision's domestic ministries. The local affiliates, however, retained their independence.

With the greater funding base and organizational infrastructure of World Vision, Love Inc. will be able to become proactive in targeting communities for new clearinghouses. Instead of waiting for local Christian leaders to invite us to come and make a presentation, we can now identify cities where a clearinghouse would be valuable and then seek local pastors and lay leaders who might launch one. We hope to have a prototype Love Inc. office in every state by 1997. World Vision support services and existing contacts will also enable Love Inc. to help develop educational activities and materials for church workers and to broker specific programs originating in one community to other communities which might also use them.

OVERSEEING THE ESTABLISHMENT of Love Inc. offices in more than fifty communities across the country has brought me in contact with the remarkable variety of church life in America. Despite the differences from one region to another, however, certain constants have clearly emerged from Love Inc.'s nationwide experience:

• **A natural progression of ministry.** The church is weak at serving not because it does not have the resources but because it has not been using them. The church is like someone who sits around all day and eats too much: the person may have lots of physical potential but is not in shape to do much at present. The church needs exercise. And like someone who is out of shape, the church should not try to leap up and run a ten-kilometer race. No matter how impatient we may be to have the churches move, the personal resources of the body of Christ can only be activated step by step. There is a natural progression from helping with smaller needs to helping with greater ones. Clearinghouses seem inevitably to pass through the same progression.

The *first* stage is meeting direct, simple, physical needs—needs for transportation, a job, a car to be repaired or a meal to be cooked. The *second* stage is project development. For example, after two years of working together in the Love Inc. network, twenty-six Holland-area churches established cooperative shelter care for abused women. Later, some of these same churches opened a foster-care home for developmentally disabled adults. Forty-six cooperated in developing a prison ministry. The *third* stage is relational helping—sharing living skills such as budgeting, developing relationships in which people "come alongside" the needy person, helping with chronic needs, offering friendship. These are family support system ministries.

Following this natural progression involves more than learning new skills or setting up new structures. As ministry gets more personal, more relational, the character of the care-giver becomes more important. A Christian who is a poor parent can nevertheless give a sick person a ride to the doctor, and the sick person may receive the service as blessing. But if the same Christian tries to come alongside a single mother and show her how to raise her children more effectively, the Christian parent's own problems will come to the surface and thwart the attempt at ministry. Ministry in response to simple requests does not require the degree of personal authenticity that relational, support-system ministry requires. Thus, as ministry progresses from simple services to relational caring, the importance of personal authenticity increases. Of course, so does the possibility of having a life-changing impact on the person who is helped.

• **Interdenominational cooperation.** Everywhere I go I see a remarkable variety of denominational participation. Churches of more than fifty denominations and many independent churches cooperate in Love Inc. networks. Together we focus not on political or social agendas, but on outreach in the name of Christ. On that basis, cooperation across the church spectrum is possible.

When we began, I mistakenly assumed that theologically "liberal" churches would be the primary partners in ministry. But I have found that "liberal" and "conservative" theological designations are almost totally immaterial. Mainline and evangelical Protestant churches, Roman Catholic and Orthodox churches— all are willing to cooperate so long as the shared focus is the ministry of the body of Christ to people in need.

• **Small churches as well as large can serve.** I also assumed that large churches would be the predominant partners, because they have more resources. But experience shows that every church has *some* material resources. And, more important, the real resources of churches are people. A church's *per capita* impact is not affected by the total number of its members. The smallest church in one Michigan county saw the need for food and clothing and initiated a combined ministry of churches by opening a food and clothing bank.

• **There are no celebrities or heroes.** The important actors are those church members who are actually communicating Christ's love. This ministry does not depend on endorsements by political figures or denominational offices. Everywhere it derives its strength at the grass roots, especially from laypeople.

Love Inc. clearinghouses themselves are mainly staffed by ordinary Christians. For example, while a few program directors have professional training, most are homemakers who have not had a career in the helping professions. The majority works part time; most are unpaid. While all are qualified and trained for their responsibilities, some do not have all the professional skills that might enable them to lead their Love Inc. affiliate to become all that, in theory, it might be. But they have the more important virtues of Spirit-filled spontaneity and commitment, a gentle spirit and a servant's heart. They are instinctively adept at managing by means of a shared vision.

• **The Holy Spirit.** Over and over I am reminded that the Love Inc. model for facilitating Christian caring cannot work without the Holy Spirit. Over and over I hear the same initial reactions: "Agencies won't cooperate." "Churches won't cooperate." "Churches and agencies won't work together." "Church members won't want to get involved." "You'll never find the money—or the board—or the staff—or the office." Humanly speaking, these factors seem likely to defeat any attempt to set up a clearinghouse. And so every success has to be attributed to the power of the Holy Spirit.

TWELVE YEARS OF TESTING the Love Inc. model have taught some practical lessons about the ministry of Christian caring. A few in particular are worth mentioning here:

• A single Love Inc. office cannot take on an entire major metropolitan area such as Chicago or Detroit. An early attempt to do so in Chicago foundered. But later efforts have demonstrated that it is possible to focus on a neighborhood or area within a large city. Cities, in fact, are composed of neighborhoods. A Love Inc. clearinghouse can develop a balance of needs and resources in a particular section of a metropolitan area.

• Love Inc. clearinghouses must be constantly on guard against the tendency of churches to create central helping services not integrated with the church itself. There is a powerful temptation to retreat from a dependence on the time and talents of church members and to return to an approach that depends on professionals supported by the donations of church members. In one city the churches affiliated with Love Inc. held a huge combined garage sale to raise money for a contingency fund for Love Inc., to expedite the relief process. But then, whenever Love Inc. tried to make referrals involving material resources to churches, the churches responded that they expected Love Inc. itself to provide help through the contingency fund. Thus an approach that was sound from an administrative and bureaucratic point of view was destructive of ministry involving many church members. Love Inc. must constantly hold up the vision of ministry by church members. An insert in the February 14 bulletin of one Denver church encouraged me creatively along this line. The church's contact person, Debby Paulson, sent it. It celebrated some of the small but significant acts of concern that church members performed—see pages 172-173.

• As churches reach out, they are forced to confront two questions about their own church life: Are you ready to grow? Are you willing to be joined by people who are different? Christian caring reveals the love of Christ, and people respond. The local church body must consider whether it is prepared to welcome those who do. Staying small and staying the same may be more comfortable. But what do you say to people of a different color or social background who have met Christ through your ministry and want in to your church?

• The group in the church least mobilized for ministry is successful homemakers. They have a great range of skills required for Christian caring. Many also meet the qualifications for staffing Love Inc. clearinghouses— administration, scheduling, budgeting, planning, problem-solving, evaluating, coordinating multiple needs. It will be a tragic loss if the churches fail to recognize their abilities—and availability—and do not give them the help they need to hone their skills.

THE GREATEST LESSON TO BE learned from the first dozen years of Love Inc. is that there is in principle

LOVE NOTES FROM LOVE INC.

- **Randy Pickering** tested a lady's car free of charge and helped refer her to a location for inexpensive parts.

- **Phillip Dulmage** fixed a refrigerator for some people who had relied on a fan behind it to keep it cool for over one year.

- **Neil Chen** towed a car all the way from Lakewood to Aurora for a family and a newborn son who were moving from a shelter to a rental house. The Robertsons donated a crib, a playpen, a walker and baby toys to this same family.

- **Mike Mitchell** helped an elderly couple replace and repair a gutter damaged by the snow.

- **Bree Eddy** and her son went over to an elderly man's house to help him fill out his property/rent/heat rebate forms. Bree was concerned about the gentleman's health and a follow-up call is assuring that he gets proper medical care.

- **Mary Miller, Cindy Sullivan and Debby Paulson** made cookies for a Love Inc. fund-raiser.

- **Debby Paulson** has made numerous calls to a paraplegic, severely depressed man to offer support.

- **Tom Gallinger** offered advice to a lady who needed a gas line installed.

- **Ed Callaghan** took a food basket (prepared by the In Jesus' Name Shelter and Ed's wife, **Lois**) to a single lady and her four children. Ed also took an elderly lady to a doctor's appointment.

- **Debby Paulson** took a food basket assembled by the In Jesus' Name Shelter to an elderly couple in ill health.

- **Randy Fowler** helped a man and a woman move and was able to witness effectively to them with compassion and experience.

- **Scott Paulson, Don Letton and Don Thornton** helped a single lady and her two children move from a house, from which they were evicted, to a more manageable housing project. **Ellen and Blanton Donaldson** loaned their truck to help.

- **Don Letton** also helped a lady from the church move.

- **Scott Paulson** and his family helped an evicted family move to In Jesus' Name Shelter and then to an apartment after they had

172

saved some money.

- **Bob Williams** made a house call to an elderly bed-ridden lady who could not find any other medical personnel to come to her.

- **Debby Paulson** took care of a ten-month-old baby for five hours while his single father took a break.

- **Louise Wright** provided transportation to a lady in order for her to take her driver's test.

- **Gary Baughman** fertilized a lawn for an elderly lady of the church. He also computerized the volunteer information for **Love Inc.** and assisted with the preparation of this newsletter.

- **Ken and Georgia Polsley** graciously offered their home to a couple from the shelter for two weeks.

THANKS TO YOU ALL! YOUR COMMITMENT TO HELP AND LOVE OTHERS IS OVERWHELMING.

WHAT IS LOVE INC.?

Love Inc. means **"Love in the name of Christ."** The **Love Inc.** church services network works with the Christian churches in the Denver metropolitan area to help show God's love to needy people in practical ways. The program is based on the premise that the resources to meet any need can be found in the body of Christ and that, working together, the people in that body can make a significant difference in our communities.

Love Inc. began in 1981 in Holland, Michigan, and has now grown to more than forty active chapters nationwide. The Denver area program began in 1987. At Bear Valley Church, the **Love Inc.** representative is Debby Paulson. **Love Inc.** serves as a liaison between needy individuals, public and private organizations and churches. It helps reduce duplication of community services and works to unleash the potential of previously untapped volunteer and material resources within churches.

If you would like to contribute your talents for the good of others through **Love Inc.**, please contact Debby Paulson at 989-5257.

Bulletin, Bear Valley Baptist Church, Denver, Colorado
Frank Tillapaugh, pastor

no divinely ordained limit to the needs that the church can take on. And the most important limitation in practice does not lie in shortages of people or material resources in the church, for these are very great. The most severe limitation is our preconceived notions of what the church can and cannot do.

Recently I had a conversation with a friend of mine who is a realtor. "Do you believe that the body of Christ can respond to all human needs?" I asked him.

"Without question," he replied.

"Do you think it should have a role in providing shelter—caring for transients, for the homeless, making home ownership possible for the poor?"

"That's not the role of the church," he said.

"Then," I told him, "you will have to show me where in the New Testament there is an exclusionary clause."

As church members have responded to needs, simple and complex, material and emotional, it has become apparent that God's vision for the ministry of the church is much bigger than mine. I believe that the call of Love Inc. is not only to facilitate the engagement of church members in ministry, but even more to say to the church, "Reshape your expectations for what Christian ministry can do. Open your eyes to see the full ministry that God is giving to the body of Christ."

Everywhere you look in society today there are people with needs. Caught between the disintegration of families and family networks on the one hand, and reductions in government spending on the other, many people's needs will not be met unless they find help from the body of Christ. By God's grace, Christ's people do have the solutions to the problems our neighbors face. I am convinced that Christ will allow us to confront no need for which His church does not have the appropriate resources to respond.

I believe this even though at present relatively small numbers of church members are actively engaged in Christian caring. God has never needed large numbers of people to accomplish His will in the world. That is the lesson of Gideon, in the book of Judges. He assembled a fighting force of 32,000 men to confront the Midianites. Not impressed, God thinned the ranks by dismissing the 22,000 (sixty-nine percent) who were timid and afraid. Later He reduced the number by another 9,700 (thirty percent), leaving a hesitant Gideon with only 300 soldiers. God gave Gideon victory with less than one percent of the troops he began with. And his triumph was so great that afterward the nonparticipants actually complained that they had not been involved.

The same principle applies today. God can easily use the same percentage of church members to change our communities. If a church has 500 members, God can use five to develop a successful ministry. The success of this caring core will inevitably attract other people, who may have been hesitant to participate in the initial stages of the caring ministry. The critical factor is not size or numbers. Gideon's tiny band of men encountered success because they had a unified purpose and an organizational plan, both of which were dedicated to God's praise. They knew what they had to do and they knew how to do it. Successful church ministries possess the same ingredients. It is exciting to see that the body of Christ is beginning to awaken to its calling and empowerment to minister in Christ's name.

Stung by a Song

A SONG BY KEITH GREEN pricked Charlotte Reeves's conscience. Green sang about the picture Jesus gave of the final judgment, when He will say that whatever we neglected to do for the least of His brothers, we neglected to do for Him. Jesus gives us opportunities to serve Him, the song went, but often we fail to take them.

Charlotte had always served in the church—teaching Sunday school, playing piano with a group of women who traveled to give Christian concerts, giving lay counseling to other women. But Keith Green's song touched a sore spot—her awareness that she was always ministering *in* the church, never *outside* it.

"The closest I came to the poor," she once told me, "was playing the piano occasionally at a rescue mission. I had an incredible desire to do something for

177

underprivileged people, but I didn't know how. I lived in a middle-class neighborhood, and I never saw them."

Charlotte needed some means for getting outside the church walls. She needed a link with the needy.

The clue came in Michael McManus's syndicated column reporting on Love Inc. Charlotte wrote me and asked if I would come to Bakersfield, California, to explain Love Inc. to Christians in her city. I agreed to come.

For Charlotte, the invitation was a step of faith. She had no way of knowing whether anyone would show up for such a meeting. But with the help of her daughter, she sent out invitations to all the pastors in town.

Fewer than ten came. I explained what Love Inc. is all about. Afterward, over coffee, I told Charlotte she should not be discouraged by the small turnout. Numbers don't mean anything, I said. But I told her I didn't think anything would happen unless she took action.

Charlotte decided she would. She got the training materials and audio tapes that Love Inc. provides to groups setting up a clearinghouse. She helped lead a small planning committee through the steps of forming a legal corporation, meeting with agency representatives, contacting pastors and locating facilities and funding.

"About forty people came to the agency meeting," Charlotte recounts. "The board chairman and I gave presentations, and the agency people were extremely encouraging. I had never done such a thing before. Always when I had spoken I memorized a script. If I forgot it, I was lost. This time I just explained the program from notes. When we met with the pastors, I fielded questions. The Lord removed any fear of dealing with people.''

The response from the pastors was hardly overwhelming. Of the thirty-five who heard her presentation, only seven agreed to work with the program. But Charlotte was not discouraged. "There was no reason for them to give us credence," she observes philosophically. "We were going to have to build it."

It took more than a year of groundwork before the Bakersfield Love Inc. opened its doors and began taking calls in early 1986. Since then, filling the role of program director has meant a whole new set of responsibilities for Charlotte—developing relationships with pastors and lay leaders, strategizing about how to make contact with the resources of the churches, dealing with people who have a wide variety of needs. The Bakersfield Love Inc. has been especially active in offering budget counseling and training budget counselors. "Budget counseling will uncover all kinds of other needs in people's lives," Charlotte says. "There will be help, if they want it," she adds confidently.

How has her involvement with Love Inc. affected her? "I trust God more now," Charlotte says. "I have seen Him work so many times to meet people's needs.

"It has also raised my consciousness of God's love for the poor," she says. "I have no trouble turning people down who, I believe, are abusing the system. But as I have listened to stories of genuine need, it has made me sensitive to pain and suffering, especially of women. It has opened my eyes to the total failure of the sexual revolution. It has also made me feel compassion for men who don't fulfill the male role to provide for their families.''

The personal challenge of approaching pastors, heads of agencies, and civic leaders is not something that Charlotte would ever have envisioned herself doing. "I would not have been comfortable with that, formerly," she says. "But the ability to do it has been there. I have never even thought about it; it has just happened. The Bible refers to power from the Holy Spirit. I can honestly say I have experienced it. The tiny steps of faith that I have taken to respond to the Lord and get involved have unleashed God's power.''

Charlotte looks to new ministry challenges. While she is unsure whether she should remain as program director, her life has taken a new direction. "It has been so good to be part of a body of Christians who are reaching out to hurting people. I am convinced now, more than ever before, that God's love is the answer to the suffering of our culture.''

ELEVEN

What Lies Ahead?

IT WOULD BE PRESUMPTUOUS to predict the future of Christian caring. But it is possible to say a little about what may lie ahead for Love Inc. and the churches that are sharing in ministry through it. Here is what I foresee:

• **Churches will establish congregational clearinghouses.** So far Love Inc. has focused on developing community-wide clearinghouses. Each clearinghouse links helping agencies and churches and opens the way for individual church members to enter into ministry. While establishing new clearinghouses in targeted cities will be a major concern, in the next few years we will also be working to involve churches in ministering to needs in localities where it is not possible at present to set up a community-wide clearinghouse.

We are beginning to help individual churches develop

clearinghouses within their own congregations. The model we are developing will help a church identify needs in conjunction with area agencies and then deploy its resources. It will also enable a church to coordinate all its various ministries. A pilot project is underway at Lansing, Michigan, with the cooperation of Pastor Greg Wood at Trinity United Methodist Church. When the congregation was surveyed for talents, 290 of the 600 people in attendance indicated their willingness to minister, marking an average of three ministry areas each. Our goal is to help the church structure its ministries so that services to prisoners, shut-ins, the hungry, and so on are coordinated with each other and draw on the largest possible number of volunteers. When this model is developed, we will have something to offer to individual churches that want to involve their members in ministry but cannot find enough other churches in their area to set up a community-wide clearinghouse.

In addition, for individuals who desire ministry but whose churches are not interested in the clearinghouse approach, we are beginning to develop member ministry videos that will give them individual training.

• **Churches will grow in their capacity to** *discover* **needs, not merely** *respond* **to them.** Now only the more vocal needs are met. Churches are reactive. But Christ did not sit in the temple and wait for people to come to Him. Most of His healings took place as He was moving among the people. Churches should imitate their Master, going beyond a passive response to people in need, to seek out those who are hurting.

Love Inc. hopes to expand systematically the

awareness of churches of what they can do to seek out needs. We are developing ways to teach church contact people not only how to inventory the resources of their congregations so that they can respond to requests for help, but also how to discover and diagnose the needs of people in their churches and neighborhoods.

Our approach uses the analysis grid that is shown on page 184. The grid does not immediately identify needy people. Rather it helps volunteers understand those whose situation makes them vulnerable and trains them in finding out whether these vulnerable people are actually in need. The grid employs five biblical categories—the weak, prisoners, strangers, widows and orphans—and gives these categories some contemporary applications. For example, for "strangers" we might think of refugees; for "widows and orphans," single-parent families. It then suggests the kinds of mental, physical, emotional and spiritual needs that people in each category would tend to encounter. The listing of possible needs guides a church volunteer in interviewing people in each category of potential need and checking on their situation.

Pastor Wood in Lansing is using the approach in his own congregation to call people in their neighborhoods, through an outreach called Phone Friend Network. Volunteers offer information about the church and ask a few questions, using the grid. A volunteer might say to an elderly person, "I know other elderly people who sometimes need help with grocery shopping. I wondered if that might be the case with you." If so, the churches seek to supply the need through the Love Inc. network.

BIBLICAL NEEDS IN OUR DAY

		WEAK							WIDOWS				ORPHANS					PRISONERS				STRANGERS			
		Elderly	Shut-ins	Handicapped	Mentally ill	Dev. disabled	Sick	Substance abusers	Widows	Widowers	Single parents	Divorced parents	Children	Fatherless	One parent	Runaways	Abused/neglected	Prisoners	Prisoner's fam.	AFC residents	Nursing home res.	Refugees	Transients	Street People	Homeless families
SPIRITUAL	Counseling																								
	Fellowship																								
	Bible study																								
	Prayer																								
MENTAL	Communication skills																								
	Legal																								
	Problem-solving																								
	Parenting skills																								
	Budget skills																								
	Advocacy																								
EMOTIONAL/ SOCIAL	Counseling																								
	Security																								
	Self-esteem																								
	Work																								
	Helping others																								
	Visitation																								
	Babysitting/day care																								
	Friendship																								
PHYSICAL	Clothing/shoes																								
	Shelter																								
	Household items																								
	Nutrition																								
	Personal items																								
	Health																								
	Rides																								
	Financial																								
	Repairs																								
	Seasonal																								

The grid helps church members to recognize needs as they arise. As information comes in through the phone network, the churches can form a profile of their congregations and neighborhoods. The categories of the grid then define target groups for ministries that the churches may consider undertaking.

• **New tools will enable churches to minister in depth to a wide range of needs.** Individuals, churches and Love Inc. networks in various localities have developed projects that are of potential use elsewhere. Love Inc. will be increasingly active in "brokering" these projects to other clearinghouses and churches. We will assist in adapting the projects for use in other communities and then will help Christians in those other communities implement them. Among the projects being developed at present to facilitate the ministries of churches are these:

★ The Domestic Violence Project. Spouse abuse is one of the needs that most of us would prefer not to acknowledge or discuss. But our reluctance to confront it will not make it go away. It is estimated that some form of physical or emotional abuse occurs in fifty percent of American homes. But while the last decade has seen the establishment of shelters and programs for abused spouses and children, there are only eighteen recovery programs for abusing spouses in the entire nation. Paul Hegstrom in Quincy, Illinois, has designed a program for abusing spouses that has had a seventy-percent success rate. Half the abusing spouses who have been served through the program have turned their lives over to Christ. Two churches, one in Kansas and the other in Michigan, are testing the program. When it becomes generally available, it will give any church of at least a hundred members a tool for serving abusing spouses, thus filling a need for healing and reconciliation that can only be found in the body of Christ.

★ A Community Marriage Policy. In response to the high rate of divorce among the Christians who made their marriage vows in local churches, Pastor Jim Talley encouraged pastors of more than sixty congregations in Modesto, California, to develop a marriage preparation policy. Pastors agreed to require any couple wanting to be married—whether young or old, charter members of a church, pregnant, or whatever—to complete four months of instruction in the marriage relationship. The churches allow only couples who participate in the program to take marriage vows.

The results are impressive. For example, over the course of ten years 700 couples have asked Talley to be married. But after taking the program, half have decided not to marry. Among the 350 who have married, none has gotten divorced. The Love Inc. program in Fresno, California, has adapted the policy, and it has already been signed by more than eighty-five pastors in that community. Soon a video presentation explaining the approach will be generally available. Love Inc. believes that this church-based preventive ministry can reduce divorce by up to fifty percent in any community.

★ A Budget-planning Curriculum. Love Inc. affiliates in Bakersfield, California, and Allendale, Michigan, have developed an experimental program to train church volunteers in giving ongoing budgeting instruction and support to people with chronic financial problems. The prototype will soon be tested by churches elsewhere in the country.

★ Project Home Again. The program was originated by World Vision to invite churches to draw on the model of refugee sponsorship for Indo-Chinese immigrants and develop a similar relationship with homeless families. The program involves highly structured training for the program director and church representatives. Church volunteers provide a wide variety of supportive services, introducing hope in a situation that is often devoid of hope.

• **Training for pastors.** We are developing a three-hour workshop titled "How to Handle the Poor at Your Church Door." The program will educate pastors, outreach workers and church secretaries in how to analyze needs and mobilize church members. Of course it will recommend the establishment of a clearinghouse in the community. But where that is not possible at present, it will give church leaders usable strategies. The program will be especially useful for seminarians. Young pastors who have not been prepared to deal with the sometimes manipulative individuals who appear at the church's door too often follow a pattern of reckless enthusiasm to serve followed by cynical refusal to respond to any need. It is hoped that the Love Inc. program will offer those who are about to step into pastoral responsibilities some early wisdom to forestall this problem.

LOOKING BEYOND LOVE INC. to the ministry of churches, I believe we will see churches growing in their capacity to address the needs of children, single families and the elderly. For me, one of the most compelling biblical images regarding need is the picture of children clustered around Christ. What did they talk about? I suspect that their conversation with Jesus quickly turned from childish trivia to shadowy areas of pain and despair. Certainly that would be true today, given the abuse, neglect and homelessness that so many children suffer. In Los Angeles alone, there are presently 1,400 children living in skid row hotels.

Secular agencies have tried valiantly but in vain to meet the needs of children in pain. Christ might even commend them for their attempts. I am convinced that He now challenges the churches to address the needs of children. For many children, there is no alternative to the church. If authentic Christian fathers and mothers do not get down on knees, reach out and embrace them with the love of Christ, they will not find help anywhere.

The vast majority of poor in America are children and single mothers. The welfare system, despite good intentions, effectively consigns them to perpetual neediness. As young single women born in poverty mother a new generation of children, a situation of economic and emotional deprivation is created from which many believe they can never escape. For these people, the only effective outreach is that which focuses on their value as persons and gives them the living skills to overcome their situation.

The groups at the ends of the life span—children and the elderly—are most vulnerable in our society today. I believe the churches will grow in their ministry to both in the years ahead.

I also see churches increasingly celebrating the ministry of their members. I expect we will see churches incorporating members' experience of ministry in preaching and religious education. The divorce between Christian teaching within the church and Christian ministry outward from the church will be overcome. When churches teach, "Thou shalt love thy neighbor," they will offer examples of Christian caring and opportunities to participate in it.

The pressures of church members entering into ministry will reshape church life. Consider a congregation like St. Paul United Methodist Church in Fairbanks, Alaska, pastored until recently by the Rev. Paul Wilcox. St. Paul Church had seventy-two members, more than forty of whom were actively providing transportation, emergency shelter, food bank services, housework and home maintenance, rental assistance and nursing home services. A congregation like that will expect preaching and education that will prepare and celebrate their engagement in ministry. Now that we're involved in all this, church members will say, give us the help we need to do it well. A pastor who does not get down to that level of equipping and affirming will find that he is not keeping pace with his congregation.

In many individual Christians I sense a restlessness, a growing need to express and apply their faith. Church members are demanding the right to graduate to ministry. If a few churches now demand a written commitment that members will engage in ministry, in the future we may see many churches where members demand

189

tangible opportunities to demonstrate the love of Christ. They will want educational programs that teach them how to care, how to share living skills effectively, how to translate their giftedness into practical application.

My Favorite Volunteer

IN ALL THE YEARS of working with church members, my favorite volunteer is a woman in her mid-sixties. For a long time, whenever I would speak with her, she would talk about friends who had died and about her arthritis. She also talked wistfully about a great disappointment in her life. As a girl she had set her goal to become a teacher, to train children and share Jesus Christ with them. But she came from a poor family, and after the eighth grade she was required to go out to work to help support her family. Later she married, and then she sometimes had to work outside the home to supplement her husband's earnings and sometimes stayed at home and cared for her four children. She never regretted any of this, but she wondered what might have been.

I approached this woman one day and said that we

needed tutors for Hispanic and Oriental children. "Will you tutor?" I asked. In effect, I was asking, Will you become the teacher you always wanted to be?

"I can't," she replied. "I'm too old."

"You're not too old," I replied.

"I don't have the skills," she objected.

"I'll train you," I said.

She finally agreed to go through the training program—probably to get me off her back. But she told me she wasn't planning to tutor; she would just help in other ways. "Fine," I said.

At the end of the training, I asked her to tutor two Hispanic boys. She gave in.

In subsequent months, when I saw her, I would ask, "How is your arthritis?"

"What?" she would say. Instead, she would tell me about the boys.

"Have you been reading the obituaries lately?" I would ask.

"No," she would answer, and then tell me about the problems the boys were having. The boys became her life.

A week before Christmas she was sitting in her living room, and she heard a terrible commotion outside. When she opened the front door, there stood the two boys in the snow. They had brought all their classmates to sing Christmas carols to their "favorite teacher."

It is hard to imagine that anyone anywhere was happier that night. She had become the teacher she had wanted to be.

I often think that this woman, who is my mother, is

like many other people in the church: all reticence and excuses, but when they get the right opportunity, the training and the encouragement, they succeed.

Checklist for Church Ministry

Here is a list of questions to help in evaluating your own church's ministry to needy neighbors:

1. Can you name one individual or family helped by any organizations your church supports?

2. Does your church have a system for anticipating needs of church members, or do staff people wait to find out what people need?

3. Can you list the three primary needs in your own community? What are they?

   _____

   _____

4. Have you been asked in the last two years to respond to a specific need for a named individual or family?

5. Can you identify your own favorite volunteer experience? Share it.

   _____

   _____

6. Does your church have a mission statement? Please discuss it.

   _____

   _____

7. Does your church give public recognition to the contributions of volunteers?

8. Does anyone other than your pastor or other official church leaders respond to needs in the church?

9. Does your pastor illustrate in teaching and preaching each Sunday what it means to love your neighbor?

10. Can you name the three neighbors of your church?

11. Can you name the children in your own three neighboring homes?

12. Are the ministries of your church coordinated with each other?

Setting Up A Clearinghouse

These are the steps for setting up a Love Inc. clearinghouse in a community:

1. Please contact Love Inc., P.O. Box 1616, Holland, MI 49422. Love Inc. will send you information about the ministry and offer a ten-minute video tape, "A Love Story."

2. Love Inc. shares a presentation describing the ministry with church and agency representatives from your community.

3. Love Inc. equips a planning committee, composed of seven to twelve representatives from at least eight different churches, to identify a board of directors, designate the program director (or directors) and prepare the groundwork for the ministry.

4. Love Inc. orients the president of the board of directors and trains the program director to establish relationships with community service providers, develop office procedures and present the program to pastors.

5. The program director shares Love Inc. with area service providers and develops interagency policies and procedures.

6. The program director presents the Love Inc. program to area pastors.

7. Love Inc. trains the program director to develop a church services network.

8. The program director trains contact people from the participating Love Inc. churches.

9. The contact people from each church present the ministry within their churches and enlist volunteers.

10. The Love Inc. clearinghouse begins to link needy people with church members.